PRAISE FOR *EN*

MW01256208

"*Refreshingly honest, and always thought-provoking, this diverse collection of voices will stay with readers as they walk the paths of their own careers.*"
JANE URQUHART
Internationally acclaimed Canadian author and poet

"*I'm going to use a word that captures how I felt after reading the first couple of pages - WOW! Then after reading the first couple of chapters - PHENOMENAL!*"
JENNIFER SLAY
Co-Founder All Women L.E.A.D.

"*Reading stories of the personal journeys of these amazing women leaders and the unjust systemic obstacles and societal challenges they faced, left me feeling very frustrated, sad, angry, and disappointed. We still have a long way to go to ensure equitable, diverse, and inclusive workplaces.*"
LIEUTENANT GENERAL (RETIRED) GUY THIBAULT, OMM, MSC, CD
Former Vice Chief of the Defence Staff,
Canadian Armed Forces

"*Thoughtful consideration and discussion of each of these stories by board members, C-suite executives, organizational leaders at all levels, and human resources professionals would move organizations forward toward more equitable and just environments.*"
MARLENE JANZEN LE BER, PHD, CHE
Professor, Leadership Studies Distinguished Chair,
Centre for Leadership Brescia University College

"This book reads like a series of short, poignant stories, captivating my imagination and causing me to travel to a place of deep reflection. I found the book both affirming and validating. It affirmed that we as women are not alone in our journey, and we should more intentionally share our experiences and connect more."

SEQUETTA F. SWEET, ED. D.
Assistant Professor of Organizational Leadership,
Stockton University

"It stands as a testament to the enduring legacy of women leaders and a clarion call for a more inclusive, equitable future. A must read!"

DR. ZAINUB VERJEE, C.M.
Executive Director of Galleries Ontario/Ontario Galleries,
Sr. Fellow Massey College, University of Toronto, McLaughlin
College Fellow at York University

"A crisply written compilation of stories. The book is a combination instructional manual – including questions – and biographical sketches. The message – harness your ambition, stick to your goals and, you, too can be recognized as a leader."

KARIN WELLS
Acclaimed journalist and lawyer

"This book highlights so many familiar obstacles, yet each story gives the reader a sliver of hope in overcoming barriers and owning your leadership journey. It's a timely and necessary read."

SOLANGE TUYISHIME KEITA
President & CEO - Elevate International

"Mitchell is commended for presenting these personal stories, allowing readers to relate and learn from them, supporting women on their paths of self-discovery and management success."

BRENDA CHARTRAND

Executive Coach President, Primebridge Consulting Inc.

"I appreciate this book's personal stories and experiences that highlight the importance of self-awareness, collaboration, and persistence when it comes to mindful leadership."

MEENA DAS

CEO, NamasteData

"Embracing Ambition is the guidebook every woman working as a leader - or who aspires to lead - has been waiting for; assembling the inspiring real-life journeys of a dozen leaders into a single volume that we can turn to for advice, guidance, and motivation."

EMMA LEWZEY

Founder and CEO Blue Sky Philanthropy

EMBRACING AMBITION

FOREWORD BY DAHLIA LITHWICK

EMBRACING AMBITION

Empowering Women to Step Out, Be Seen, & Lead

VOICES OF BOLD LEADERS

JENNY MITCHELL
EDITOR AND CO-AUTHOR

MIMBRES PRESS
of Western New Mexico University

MIMBRES PRESS
of Western New Mexico University

Mimbres Press of Western New Mexico University
www.mimbrespress.wnmu.edu

Media and Publisher Inquiries:

Mimbres Press of WNMU
1000 West College Ave.
Silver City, NE 88062

Cover and interior design GKS CREATIVE
Editing by Shelley Chung and Cindy Doty

978-1-958870-12-9 (hardcover)
978-1-958870-11-2 (paperback)
978-1-958870-13-6 (ebook)

FIRST EDITION

First printed in the United States

Library of Congress Case #1-13439338661

CONTENTS

FOREWORD

To (very broadly) paraphrase Tolstoy, happy leaders are all the same, but genuine, complicated, and authentic *female* leaders, well, now they are wildly interesting. Women seeking and assuming compensated, titled, authoritative leadership roles is a sufficiently novel proposition in the long sweep of human history, that too many of us still feel like we are inventing the form on the fly. And because there is no established template for it; no tried-and-true airport-book formula for succeeding at being an ambitious, successful, powerful professional woman, it can also feel like the loneliest happy ending in the myth of the American Dream.

In part because women were not designed to be lonely at the top, the imperative to candidly share stories, tactics, lessons –and—above all—missteps is strong among women leaders, as is the need to smooth the way for the women who will follow. In the coming pages you will encounter the abundant, generous, and honest voices of women who have achieved the pinnacle of leadership in their respective professional lives: in the corporate and philanthropic worlds, in the service industry in the arts, and in the law. And what they most urgently want you to understand is that almost any book that opens with a singular, linear prescription for professional success as a woman was probably neither intended for women, nor written by one.

It's complicated.

The women who share their stories here talk openly about stumbling blocks and sabotage, about systemic racism and sexism and xenophobia at the highest echelons of those same corporate and academic institutions that purport to be attempting to eradicate them. The ambitious leaders in these pages talk about answering to boards that move too slowly, and to the consequences of a global pandemic that shifted everything in the blink of an eye. They talk about fair compensation, and the lack thereof. They remind us—with bracing clarity—of what it means to be told, over and over, that you are an invaluable and irreplaceable member of a professional team, and yet lack some essential, logical character trait that could ever allow you to lead it. Each of the women sharing her story here tells of picking her way through all the challenges and the naysayers and the bullies and the limited fields of vision, to succeed, and succeed again, even as they remind us that professional success on its own terms may look very different in the rearview mirror, with the benefit of sometimes *years* of journeying.

Perhaps the most striking through line in this richly woven tapestry of women and willing to live their way into their own ambition, is how very crowded their lives are; teeming with the voices of the partners who move across the country to support them, the children who both deplete and complete them, the mentors who shape them, and the teams who look up to them, even on the days they feel themselves tripping over the starting line. Every woman in this book is carrying a whole entire world in her earbuds, every day, and they share with us the fact that the voice they hear constantly, cranked up to do maximalist damage, is the voice telling them that they don't belong here, they don't deserve this, that they were the authors of their own missteps, and that they will surely be caught out at any moment as the failures they know themselves to be.

This book is loud with the voices that tell women in leadership positions to be more nurturing and also less emotionally available, more hands-on and yet less micromanaging, more visionary and also more conservative; to be more collaborative and less so.

So many of the women you will meet in these pages describe what it takes to distill all of these messages and warnings into a single voice: The crystalline, small voice that is their own. Whether it takes the form of a "depression hammock," or a series of letters to herself, or the faint echo of a grandmother's wisdom, the true arc of so many of the women leaders profiled here takes them back to their own selves, buried under a pile of leadership books and cultural norms and road rules written by those who have never imagined a woman boss or never learned from one.

Ultimately, the alchemy in evidence here is the realization that being a powerful woman is not really the final goal. The end in itself is not the dream job, nor the pencil skirt nor the accolades, or even the announcement of your new title at a swanky European event (although such things are delicious and should be plentiful and abundant). What emerges from the panoramic swirl of expe-rience, failure, cutbacks, awkward negotiations, slights, fights, and triumphs, is that the women who dream of being leaders and the women who come to soar in their fields never do it alone. It is in this cacophony of truths, the tumult of mentorship and advice and course correction, in the shared wisdom and experience, that women find their way to the top. Reading the accounts of these ambitious leaders, one comes away with the sense that it is their candor, and their curiosity, and their vulnerability, that will light the way to a uniquely new and powerful way of being in which women can lead together, celebrate one another, and lift one another up along the way. The very telling of these stories is a promise that our daughters will someday require fewer maps and guides, and many more pencil skirts and corner offices.

—**DAHLIA LITHWICK,** Senior Editor, Slate.
New York Times bestselling author of *Lady Justice: Women, the Law, and the Battle to Save America*

INTRODUCTION

In 2022, I attended an international conference where I had a completely unexpected out-of-body experience. It happened during a presentation by Dr. Meghan Rehbein in which she presented the findings from her doctoral research. The research itself explored the lived experiences of highly successful women CEOs who managed very large budgets and complex organizations with large workforces.

During her time at the podium, Dr. Rehbein used those lived experiences to inform and describe five key pillars she had identified as consistent across the leadership journeys of these women leaders.

I went in expecting to be interested. What I did not expect was to feel so *seen*. With each description, I felt like she was describing, with specific details, my life, my leadership journey, my lived experience. I found myself nodding along as she spoke and wondering how she could possibly be talking about me when she didn't even know me. I had to keep reminding myself that she was presenting data, not telling my life story!

From the podium, Dr. Rehbein articulated themes I had felt but had never been able to put actual words to. She described situations that I assumed were unique to my experience but, as it turns out, were common threads across the experiences of many women leaders.

That presentation planted the seeds for this book by sparking an idea that shifted the trajectory of my life and my work, renewing my commitment to supporting women leaders not only with coaching, community, and strategies, but also with information, research, and data supporting their journey to the C-suite. The thesis of the idea is this: we can, and must, do a better job of preparing women for leadership so that they may more skillfully navigate the obstacles they will inevitably encounter.

This book is a marriage of the research and the lived experiences of women leaders. I believe this symbiosis is the most supportive mechanism for accomplishing the goal of preparing women for leadership. The research proves the existence of the obstacles; and the stories, in turn, breathe life into the data, illuminating what it actually feels like to lead through and overcome these barriers.

My vision was to capture as many diverse perspectives as possible so that when people read this book, they see themselves in the stories. Just like that day when I heard Dr. Rehbein's research presentation, I wanted women to "nod along" as they read these stories so they would know that they are not alone— that others have walked this journey and have learned from it. I set about gathering a collection of women from different backgrounds, different sectors, and different experiences.

My enthusiasm must have been infectious, because before I knew it, I had gathered twelve women CEOs from across North America to join me in Toronto in early 2023 for a weekend of story development, writing workshops, and connection.

And this is perhaps the most important aspect of this book, one that sets it apart: we wrote this book together. What does that mean? While each of us wrote our own individual chapters, the ideas for these chapters came out of our collective conversations and brainstorming during that weekend. Women are natural collaborators and it is a cornerstone of our leadership style. At one point during the weekend workshop, I looked across the room and saw the power of connection: one woman sharing her personal leadership story, and the other women nodding away, supporting her, asking key questions for clarification.

Being together. Holding space for one another. More than one woman said that the experience was incredibly healing for them. When you are in the "doing" of leadership, you rarely have the time to hit pause and reflect. One woman described the experience as "stepping off the conveyor belt of leadership" to take stock and capture a personal leadership narrative, one that will serve her going forward in her role.

An unexpected outcome of this process was the fact that almost all of the women talked about capturing their leadership story in real time (as opposed to reflecting on it upon retirement) as a tool for their leadership tool kit. I expected the stories and chapters to be an outcome. I was unprepared for how much this group of type A personalities was craving the "gift of reflection" that this process gave them. Once they had completed their chapters, there was a new sense of clarity about themselves, where they came from, and why they lead the way they do. Leadership is first and foremost about self-awareness. What better way to learn about yourself than to take the time to write a narrative of your personal leadership journey?

There was a lot of heaviness (you'll read about injustice, inequity, and heartbreak), but there was also a lot of laughter. Being in the company of people who have walked a parallel path to yours bonds you together. There were stories about deviled egg fiascos, blatant racial tokenism, and many stories about "waiting in the wings" for some other person to decide that you were ready to lead.

Our wish, as a collection of smart, diverse women from North America, is that you read these stories and the research, and spread the findings far and wide in your communities. Create book clubs. Organize leadership discussions. Talk about these challenges and these opportunities. And most importantly, let this collection of narratives inspire you to reflect on and share your own experiences.

By sharing your stories with one another, you will be changed, just like we too have been changed. Be brave and talk about how you felt, how you were perceived, and how that affected you. Be honest. Because when these stories come out of the shadows, they no longer hold us back. And you will be surprised how many people put their hands up and say, "I see myself in that story."

This is how we, as women, mentor ourselves and the next generation of leaders. By sharing your experience, you pay it forward for all of us: those who came before and those who follow in our footsteps.

Thank you for picking up this book. We've organized it so that each pillar, or research theme, has an introductory paragraph. Behind that description, you will find several stories demonstrating the lived experience of that pillar. You may note that many of the stories could easily fit into multiple pillars because leadership journeys are complex and nuanced. At the conclusion of each section, we've provided reflection questions to help you dig deeper into the material and pull out key lessons for your own journey.

Please know there is no right way to read it. You can start at the beginning and work your way through each chapter. Or you can flip to a pillar that resonates with you and read those stories.

In addition to the stories they've shared here, each woman has a dedicated episode on my podcast, *Underdog Leadership*. These interviews add depth and dimension to their narratives and expand on the insights in this book. I highly recommend tuning in, especially if a particular chapter resonates with you. You'll find QR codes at the conclusion of each section that will guide you directly to the episodes.

My wish is that you will "nod along" with us as you turn the pages of this collection of leadership stories that you now hold in your hands.

—JENNY MITCHELL, CFRE, CEC, DMA
Executive Coach
Founder, Chavender
Chavender.com

ABOUT THE RESEARCH

In 2021, I conducted research interviews with eleven women to explore their lived experiences and leadership journeys. Each woman was the CEO of a highly complex nonprofit with significant annual revenue and a large workforce who had held her role for at least two years.

My research focused on understanding how lived experiences help build leadership identity—the sense that these women could "see" themselves and others could see and acknowledge them as leaders. This research culminated in the submission of my dissertation-in-practice research project *Navigating the Labyrinth: Women's Leadership Identity and Lived Experience in Nonprofit Organizations.* I submitted this research to the faculty of the doctoral program in the Organizational Leadership program at Stockton University in October of 2021 in partial fulfillment of the requirements for my Doctor of Education degree.

From this body of work, I identified five themes, or pillars, that made up the leadership journeys of my research subjects. As I began presenting my findings across various contexts, it became clear that many female leaders identified with the pillars of my research—they, too, had been shaped by one or more of these formative experiences. Those five themes serve to anchor the book you hold in your hands.

Leadership is about how you understand, relate, and respond to the world around you. Growing your ability to consider alternate perspectives, shift your mindset, and become both more reflexive and more engaged are all ways to develop your vertical leadership capacity. Throughout our lives, we progress between these levels or stages of leadership development. It's not a one-way street—you can fall back as often as progress—but progressing from one level to the next has some key characteristics: heat experiences, colliding perspectives, and a process of sense and meaning-making.

The three-part process of heat experience, colliding perspectives, and sense and meaning-making is an experience of liminal space. When you are in the process of developing as a leader—in the crucible, as it were—you are betwixt and between two things. In a sense, you are forging a new leadership identity and becoming a new person—going from someone who may not have considered themselves, or been considered, a leader by others before.

The findings from the study demonstrated that the CEOs developed leadership identity through experiences of challenge. First, they repeatedly and consistently took on challenging or stretch roles throughout their careers. Second, they were able to face and overcome barriers that were related to their perceived ability or fit for these leadership roles. And finally, in many cases, they took on what's known as "glass cliff" roles.

These lived experiences have some commonalities. They are challenging but not impossible. They involve an element of risk. They include situations that naturally occur in organizations, such as input from, engagement with, and influence over others in the organization. And they are dependent on the leaders being willing and able to develop openness to other perspectives, being calm and not panicking in challenging situations, being able to think strategically about the situation they find themselves in, and eventually becoming comfortable enough with the discomfort that they begin to seek out their next challenge.

Thank you!

—MEGHAN REHBEIN, EDD
Dean, Douglass Residential College
Rutgers University

PERCEPTION BARRIERS

Participants overcame the perception that they were not the right fit to secure leadership roles. Barriers were internal—like imposter syndrome—but they were also external. For example, board members and the external community challenged their fit for the top role based on gender, race, economic background, sexual orientation, and more. Internally promoted candidates also had trouble with direct reports "seeing" them in a CEO role.

BOXES
by Onome Ako

IN A HIGHBROW HOTEL in a chic European city, I sat alongside my fellow CEOs in a meeting with our board members.

Most were male and white, with a scattering of women around the table.

I am near the head of the table, and it is time for my introduction. Everyone else at the table has been here before, but I am new to my position. All the important moments of my life led up to this. All eyes are on me.

"We are happy to introduce our fabulous new BIPOC CEO . . ."

Every other word is drowned out, and the walls seem to close in on me.

Fabulous. BIPOC.

These aren't my credentials. My skin color doesn't speak to my qualifications or the years of hard work I'd put in to earn a place at this table.

I feel myself shrink back into the box I'd been crammed into over and over and over again throughout my life and my career in Canada. That feeling of smallness, of feeling like you've crammed yourself into a tiny box. I had tricked myself into believing it was behind me, that I had outgrown that box since I was now the CEO of an international development organization.

I tune back into my formal introduction to the group. Maybe now will be the moment when she speaks to my accomplishments and to the qualifications that relate to things other than my skin color and my gender. She begins the next sentence with, "As an aid recipient, Onome . . ."

The lid to the box slams shut. An assumption—a mistaken one—that as a Nigerian immigrant, I must have been an aid recipient. Just another way of diminishing me, of keeping me one rung below everyone else seated at the table. I wonder if my white male peers would ever be introduced as being products of the welfare state.

It still surprised me that after all these years developing a career in Canada, my color and my gender always came first. When I started working in Nigeria, my color never stood out and was never mentioned. Being black and being a woman—those were the pieces of me that others saw first and I couldn't hide either of them. They were visible before I said anything. It was like people had defined who I was before I started speaking, and I would never break out of that box of assumptions.

I moved to Canada in 2007. I was inspired by my parents who had dedicated themselves to providing clean drinking water to the neighborhood where I grew up. I was determined to find my feet in the international development sector. I wanted to help people. I wanted to help not because they were "helpless," but because I believed that together we could make things better for our community. Together. To this day, I still see the word "help" as loaded. Who decides when we are "helping?" Is it the recipient? Or the helper? I think help is a two-way experience felt by both parties.

When I was in my thirties, I got a job in an organization that I cared deeply about. For me, it was my big break. And it became more than a job. It was my community, my family. That organization became my identity, and I was proud to announce I worked there.

My role within the organization gradually evolved to something off the beaten track: private sector engagement. It was a new territory, and I saw my opportunity to shine. And shine I did. I quickly became recognized within the global organization for bringing a unique set of skills to the work. Unfortunately, I was so good at my work that I became pigeonholed into this area of expertise which limited my opportunities for growth within the organization. When I tried to pursue other avenues, doors slammed in my face.

I began to worry that despite my qualifications, I would end up stuck in my role.

The breakthrough to my next job happened after a presentation I gave at a global conference. The VP of corporate social responsibility at a private sector organization took me aside and invited me to join their team through an opportunity: I would be seconded from my current job to work with them in the private sector. They saw my ability to switch between the not-for-profit and private sector worlds as an asset. They saw the value that I could bring to community engagement initiatives. Finally! The world was opening up in front of me and I was ready.

The months of dialogue, planning, and filing forms with HR were agonizing, but I kept my spirits high by envisioning how this role could break down barriers that existed between the for-profit and not-for-profit world. I thought often about the people who would benefit from this type of collaboration. Finally, the paperwork was finished, the stars were aligned, and my bags were packed.

And then I got the call. The whole thing was a no-go.

They gave an excuse about liability and risk relating to secondments. All I heard was another door slamming shut. The many visions that I had—packing my luggage, boarding my flight to different destinations, meeting my colleagues and community members, contributing to the organizational knowledge, the potential of huge impact—it all came crashing down, or in this case, streaming down through the tears I could not hold back. My nose dripped. I felt humiliated showing this much disappointment. I rushed to the washroom—the last cubicle, to be exact—to let out the tears.

That last cubicle was not a stranger to me. She and I had a history. The washroom stall had held space for me when I did my celebration dance upon receipt of my offer letter to be permanent staff. She had given me the courage to tell a colleague to stop making fun of my accent and stop telling me how "well" I spoke English. And she had been outraged on my behalf when I had been passed over for opportunities that I was more than qualified for. I was able to express my emotions with her after that time when a donor had assumed I was a "sponsored child." The stall held my shame surrounding other people's assumptions that my skin color meant I must only be qualified to work in customer service. There were high points, too: successfully advocating for equal pay for equal work alongside a male colleague with the same job.

Triumph and tears. That stall was my safe space where I didn't have to pretend anything. I didn't have to be anyone but all of myself. Thank goodness she was an accessible washroom; I always had enough space for my victory dances as well as my angry pacing!

My relationship with my bathroom stall continued for another year. I found my next role at another small not-for-profit. It was a leap of faith to step out and go for a new job.

§

I did not miss my bathroom cubicle at my new job. Maybe I didn't need it anymore, or maybe my personal challenges outweighed my work challenges. Work became an escape for me. It was such an escape that just a couple of hours before my daughter was born, I was in the waiting room at the hospital sending work emails! It goes without saying that I got a few phone calls from my boss suggesting I sign off and go on parental leave.

I would say that the majority of my challenges during this job were external. The same kind of issues came up. And they tended to focus on how people perceived me. For example, at events, guests would make a beeline toward me and ask: Is there a cash bar? Where can I find the washrooms? I would look back at them with a confused expression on my face. And then it would hit me: Oh! They think I am a server.

What would you do in this situation? You meet someone new at a party and you tell them you work for a not-for-profit. They ask, "Are you in customer service? Or admin?" Do you do what I did and say, "No, I lead partnerships," consciously downplaying what I actually do? How else do you respond to that? What would you do?

Sometimes my blood boils. Being in customer service is great. But that's not what I do. That's not what I have trained and sacrificed for all these years. Is this the box I will always be put in? Will it ever change? No one assumes that I am a leader.

I want to share a few more examples to demonstrate to you what women of color are up against on a daily basis.

I was volunteering with colleagues at a refugee center. One of the other volunteers came up to me and asked, "Do you like it here?" There was this awkward moment of silence. My eyes narrowed as I tried to understand her question, and it hit me. She thought I was a refugee. "I am Canadian," I tell her. She apologized profusely.

I also want to call out some unsavory stereotypes of my people that are deeply ingrained in Canadian culture. I feel the pressure to prove those stigmas wrong. Everybody has heard of the Nigerian email and phone scams. The unspoken question when I am working with my board of directors is: "Can our Nigerian CEO be trusted with the organization's money?" Financial transparency is and will always be a big thing for me. No room for questions. No room for doubts or maybes. Do I overcompensate? Probably, but I still do it.

When I came back to the workplace after the birth of my daughter, my raison d'être to build my career had a different meaning. I balanced being a new mom with my demanding job. I was suddenly aware of the legacy I was ready to impart to my daughter and girls just like her. I felt I had a role to play in breaking down the stereotypes so that the world could be a more inclusive place for her. I felt driven. I had a new "why" for my work.

I definitely questioned, like so many mothers, my ability to balance growing my career and raising my daughter. I was determined to be fully present for her. Family played a critical role. My parents left the lives they had built together for over forty-five years in my home country of Nigeria to start afresh in Canada to support me. At the time, they were seventy and seventy-one. Having them at home meant that I was able to raise my hand to take on assignments that stretched me. My success presented several growth opportunities for me, and I started to get noticed as a leader.

When the opportunity came up to put my hat in the ring for the executive director job, I went for it. As an internal candidate, I knew that I would need to demonstrate to the selection committee why I was the best candidate—not just the best internal candidate—for the job.

I remember a few key moments during the selection process. I prepared like hell for the interview, and I did not take it for granted that the job was mine. In hindsight, I also realize that having gone through the full interview process gained me the respect of my colleagues. This is priceless, and I would not have traded it for the world. Funnily enough, the interview process demonstrated to me that I was indeed ready to lead an organization as an executive director.

Landing the job felt good. It was made public at an international conference in 2019. I remember walking through the large halls of the Vancouver Convention Centre and being congratulated by former colleagues and peers. And then, in the midst of over six thousand people attending the conference, the head of my previous organization headed toward me and congratulated me. It felt surreal.

Back in Toronto, the real work began. As one of a handful of African women leading organizations in the international development sector, there was a lot at stake. There was the pressure of my actual work. There was my commitment to deliver on my mandate as the executive director while balancing internal and external expectations.

I had already cleaned up the balance sheet as executive director for the organization. I had navigated an unexpected global pandemic. I had reinvigorated my colleagues toward a common vision.

I wasn't looking for a change, but I took the recruiter's phone call when they reached out. At the same time, I was invited to step up as chair of a large membership-based not-for-profit organization. If I accepted both, my plate would be full!

The night before the application deadline for the role of CEO, I sat at my kitchen table with a council of trusted friends and family. I worried that both roles (CEO and chair of the board) would take too much from me and keep me away from my daughter too much. I worried about perception and wondered if I had the courage and stamina to continue fighting for my place at the table.

The kitchen table council meeting took place in the wake of the George Floyd murder. My loved ones reminded me that this decision didn't just affect my future. It could affect the entire community, and I had a responsibility to my community to go "all in" on this opportunity. I could demonstrate that positions of influence could be held by people of color. If one of their own could make it into a leadership position, then maybe it was possible for others to get there too. Putting my name forward to become CEO started to feel like it was part of a much bigger journey toward a more equitable leadership space for people that looked like and spoke like me.

Even today, I wear this mantle of responsibility with mixed feelings. On one hand, I am proud to stand for hope and possibility for others. On the other hand, occupying this space is very difficult. And it is exhausting. When you exist as a symbol, it can feel like that is all people see. I, the real Onome, the human inside this symbol, often feel invisible. For context, the obstacles I have in front of me as a female black woman are different from my white peers. I encounter racism, microaggressions, and bullying. I hold that mantle or responsibility with as much humility as I can, knowing that how I react to these situations will be carefully scrutinized by others. Everyone's watching. The burden is on me to overcome, not on others to adapt or shift their behaviors.

§

I became CEO of Action Against Hunger in 2021.

I'm often asked what it feels like to have arrived. I suppose people see a black immigrant in a CEO position and believe that I have somehow "made it" or reached an endpoint. And I will admit that for a second, I thought so too.

I think back to that moment, in a highbrow hotel, in a chic European town where I was introduced as a "fabulous BIPOC CEO." Having a seat at the table as CEO did not protect me from having the wind knocked right out of me. This was not the arrival I was expecting.

What I learned in the aftermath of that experience and what feels like a million other moments big and small, is this: there is no neat and tidy ending. We don't just wrap our experiences up in a bow.

Because the top of one mountain is the bottom of the next. And the next. And the next. A journey without an end, a story without a pretty "happily ever after."

While I speak from the experiences of my own journey, my journey is also a collective journey. The path I walk as a female black immigrant is different from the path you walk, but the point is that we're both walking. With determination and grit. We each come with our own intersectionalities and unique perspectives.

Some days I want to give up the journey altogether or take the easy route. A day where I'm not fighting for gender parity, dismantling harmful stereotypes, or navigating racial prejudice. But at the end of the day, I come home and I see my daughter's face.

And I know that every step I take means she gets to start that much further ahead.

So I keep walking.

TRUST
by Delphine Haslé

FROM A YOUNG AGE, I always knew I would be a leader. Maybe it's because I come from a family of strong, independent French women. Perhaps it's because my mom's greatest compliment was telling me that she never worries about me, that she always knew I would land on my two feet. Maybe it's because I genuinely believe you should trust your efforts. Actually, I was so sure of myself that I would read leadership books for new CEOs about how "you've made it—now what?" What a joke.

I had been working at the foundation for five years when the executive director announced his retirement. When the board of directors started the process of hiring his replacement, the foundation chair informed me that the executive committee would meet as a formality because the recommendation would be for me to be promoted to executive director.

After that special meeting of the executive committee, the foundation chair invited me to the executive director's office and announced that the top job was mine. He said we just needed to complete the paperwork. While it was a relief to hear the news, it was not a surprise; this succession plan has been discussed informally for over eighteen months.

As the foundation chair was coming out of the office, the chair of the host organization asked for five minutes of his time. The foundation and the host organization are committed to engaging each other in recruiting and selecting the executive director of the foundation. I did not think twice about it as they walked to a bench in the hallway just across from my office. From where I was sitting at my desk, I could not hear their thirty-minute conversation, but I could clearly see them. Their body language was unambiguous—the job would not be mine today. I was in a state of confusion.

The next day, the foundation chair told me that an ad hoc selection committee, including a representative of the host organization, would meet soon to discuss the succession plan. I was reminded again that I should not worry; the job was mine. I was now in a state of limbo. After a month, the selection committee met and decided that the executive committee could not make the recommendation directly to the board and that a full search for the position should be conducted. I was invited to put forward my application. At this point, I knew everyone involved was looking after the well-being of the organization, but it was difficult not to take it personally.

While preparing for the interview process, I was committed to myself. I knew there were two possible outcomes—either I get the job, or I quit. I could not fail because I wanted to be part of this wonderful organization that aligned so well with my core values. I wanted to create inspiring opportunities for our donors and harness the desire to create a better future for all. And I deserved the job!

I was always a hard worker and avid learner; I climbed the ladder during my career to put my best foot forward for this opportunity. As a scientist working in environmental non-governmental organizations (ENGOs), fundraising was always part of my job. There were times when our jobs were in jeopardy if the next grant was not coming. Like many professional fundraisers, I started with special events and moved my way up to major gifts and planned giving. Because of my interest in numbers and experience in small shops, I was often the liaison with the auditors and actively participated on many committees and board meetings.

Because I felt there was a gap in my education with only a master of science in chemical oceanography, I obtained my certificate in fundraising management from Algonquin College. Then I became a certified fundraising executive in 2015. I successfully completed various professional development opportunities to fill gaps in my skill set further. In addition, I had been doing much of the work of the executive director for the previous eighteen months as my boss and mentor dealt with his health and planned his retirement. Going into the interview, I knew I had the skill set, education, and experience required to be successful.

Many qualified candidates applied for the position, and three (including me) were invited for an interview. I prepared for the interview like I was an outsider. I met with friends with experience in campaign fundraising and leadership. With them, I practiced answers to typical difficult interview questions during mock interviews. On the day of the first interview, I felt so ready to win the job. It went like a dream—you know when you almost have an out-of-body experience where you look at this smart, poised, experienced woman, and you realize it's you. After a couple of rounds of interviews, I was the successful candidate. I earned my job!

Looking back, I am so grateful to the individuals who fought for a full job search. It took me a long time to see that it was not personal; everyone was behaving with the success of the organization in mind. Today, I know it was a beautiful gift because no one can question the process. I did earn the top job.

The board announced my appointment as executive director in June 2019, just in time for the launch of the silent phase of the largest fundraising campaign for our organization. The honeymoon phase was short-lived because I immediately realized that I needed to break through some limiting perception barriers. When I was promoted from a supporting role to the top job, some of the leadership volunteers did not see me as the leader of the organization because they had known me in more supportive and administrative roles. Others could not believe I could build a collaborative relationship between the foundation and the host organization because I represented a continuation of the "old ways." There were also some who were not sure if I could execute, implement, and oversee our new capital campaign with a goal that kept on growing.

When we moved ahead with a $10 million campaign, my focus shifted to closing five- to seven-figure gifts. The team was expected to more than double the annual revenue. To achieve this stretch goal, we needed to inspire a new circle of donors and meet their expectations from a leader in healthcare. As the leader of the organization, I needed to get buy-in from the board to authorize the new budget to build capacity.

In philanthropy, people give to people. Once we revised the number of donations required at each level to reach the $10 million goal, it became clear that we did not have the right people on our board. So I needed to recruit community leaders to help us reach out to their networks.

I knew it was crucial to gain the trust of my board, the host organization, and community leaders to be successful because fundraising is a team sport. I also wanted to prove everyone who was doubting me and my leadership wrong. So when I started the job that I deserved and earned, I went into action mode. My attack plan had three prongs.

Prong 1: Radically Collaborate

When I started my new role, we were embarking on the largest fundraising campaign in the history of the organization. Within the first six months, the campaign grew from $6.0 million to $8.5 to $10 million. Our goal was bold and inspiring, creating Canada's first Centre of Excellence in Frailty-Informed Care to transform care for seniors and veterans. While the team was revamping our case for support statements on the eve of the pandemic, finalizing the five-year budget, and developing our strategy and pipeline, I did a true assessment of my experience and leadership gaps to tackle this beast. It also became a great time to steward new opportunities to collaborate.

Believing in yourself and trusting your efforts are critical, but it is equally important to be true to yourself. It's essential to know your strengths and your weaknesses. Nobody can be an expert in everything. During my career, I saw too many leaders act like roosters in the boardroom—acting with too much pride and exhibiting their perceived power while shutting down the voice of everyone else. It always amazed me that they did not recognize how limiting their behavior was. I was told it comes with the top job, but

I refused to believe it. To remind me, I actually have a birdhouse with a rooster on top of it displayed in my office.

Radical collaboration is the key to success, especially in the not-for-profit sector. In my case, it meant gaining the trust of the foundation team, the C-suite of the host organization, our leadership volunteers, and ultimately our donors.

One of the first tasks as executive director was to hire my right-hand person. Once I got promoted, I left a key position vacant within the operations of our organization. In a small shop like our foundation, when we are one person down, we lose 25 percent of our workforce! Because of the tumultuous transition, I was not able to start the hiring process before my start date. Finding the right fit was crucial because I have great expectations for my team and we were on a trajectory of growth with the new campaign. Knowing my strengths and weaknesses was also essential because nobody wants two Delphines on the team!

After doing my homework and creating a list of requirements for my number two, I remember clearly calling this full-of-life fundraiser with experience in seniors' causes asking her to consider this opportunity. To this day, I am grateful I have had the chance to create a space for her to grow. As needed, we continue to engage specialists and experts to fill some of our gaps and support our efforts.

To be successful, I knew I needed to be able to count on the CEO of my host organization to inspire donors. This was new to our organization, and not everyone thought I could bring such a radical change to our organizational culture. My predecessor didn't prioritize that relationship, and he preferred to play a central and visible role in our organization's work. I see it differently. My work is best done in the background, serving as a matchmaker between the donors and the causes they care about. So I worked hard to build a relationship with the CEO of the host organization, even if it was sometimes awkward. Doing a happy dance in his office when we confirmed our first $2.0 million donation helped!

Prong 2: Seek Coaching and Mentorship

The next step was to ask for help during my time of transition from number two (the supporter) to number one (the leader). Because my salary was 40 percent lower than my male predecessor, I negotiated in my contract that the foundation pays for an executive coach for two years as I navigated my transition into my new role. (Full disclosure—Jenny Mitchell was my transition coach.) Working with her allowed me to be vulnerable without judgment.

It can indeed be lonely at the top! Working with a transition coach gave me not only access to a safe space but also a brave space. During those two years, Jenny worked with me to help me adapt to my new leadership role, manage my own high expectations and the perception of others, and uncover my true leadership style. During this transition period, I navigated the early days of the COVID-19 pandemic while working in healthcare philanthropy. My small but mighty team also experienced a total turnover while closing the largest corporate and individual gifts in the organization's history. This was a tumultuous time when I realized that planning is good, but actioning is better.

When I was promoted, I was not prepared for how my interactions would change overnight. For the first time, I realized how a leader could set the mood for the entire team. It can be energy-draining. I remember coming into the office one day after a poor night's sleep and just did not want to be that cheerleader anymore. All of a sudden, everyone around me was seeing the glass half-empty. So I got my figurative pom-pom out! This was even more important in the early days of the COVID-19 pandemic when people were questioning how safe it was to work in a long-term care home. Leadership is about inspiring, enabling, and empowering others to do their absolute best together to realize a meaningful and rewarding shared goal. But it's not easy every day! Being able to discuss my own fears and challenges with my coach or vent without it impacting the team was such a relief.

I also discovered early on that my colleagues did not see me as a peer anymore. It was surprising to me because I thought that I had created a space where everyone would have a chance to express their point of view. But all of a sudden, I noticed that team members would not question my ideas, even if they were clearly half-baked ideas! To help the team, I had to learn very fast to say, "I am thinking out loud right now," to invite them to use critical thinking and not jump into action mode after I expressed an idea—good or bad. I learned this trick from a peer and mentor at one of our executive women's breakfasts, and I only wish I'd learned it sooner.

As our campaign goal continued to grow, acknowledging my lack of experience in campaign fundraising was essential for the success of our organization. I read all about it in the books, and I participated in some of the campaign phases, but I never executed a major fundraising campaign from beginning to end. To gain the trust of the leadership volunteers and potentially our donors, I sought a campaign counsel who was willing to mentor me and coach the whole team. Finding the right fit at the right time was so important and valuable.

Not being afraid to accept that I needed help was a power move. Having a safe space helped me to successfully reach my most authentic potential in the shortest possible time. Having the right support during those early years helped me get results for my organization while becoming the leader I wanted to be.

Prong 3: Choose How You Will Show Up

Early in the transition, I needed to decide how I would show up to meet the expectations of the leadership volunteers, our donors, and my team. It was not a crisis of identity, but it took a real effort because I needed to align how people perceived me and still feel like myself. However, I felt no shame in playing the game if it meant bulldozing some of the perception barriers.

While respecting my authentic self, I needed to be mindful of how I would dress, how I would walk into a room, where I would sit, and how I would speak. Actually, this is still true these days, but it's getting easier, and it's more like a habit. Today, visualization methods help me be mindful and present in the moment.

For the first year of my tenure, I purchased a new blazer or a power dress before each board meeting. When we moved to virtual meetings, I would wear a blazer with a pair of jeans to feel like a badass warrior! Even with my new armor, I felt disoriented. My peers were telling me that I needed to wear specific brand names and shop in exclusive stores. But I detested those clothes and felt like a stranger if I wore them. On the flip side, I wore an outfit I loved to my very first seven-figure donation check presentation and ended up looking terrible in the photos. Tip of the day: do not wear animal print to a public speaking engagement! I decided then and there to hire a stylist to help me find the balance between personal expression and professional poise.

At my first board meeting as executive director, I served everyone coffee and helped with the room setup. I thought it would be a nice gesture. One female director who is a well-respected CEO and a renowned advocate for strong women took me aside and told me that bringing the coffee undermined my authority as a leader. I'm a team player, and I genuinely believe no matter my title, there is no job beneath me, but from that day on, I followed her advice. I sat at the head of the table and let my staff distribute the photocopies, run the PowerPoint, and bring the coffee. At that time, I realized that we still have a long way to go, and many of the stereotypes of the *Mad Men* era were still so ingrained in our society.

I can't tell you how often senior executives give unsolicited advice that people would like me more if I shower them with compliments. I decided early in my journey that I would say what I mean and mean what I say. For me, showing up authentically means being candid and speaking honestly. When I praise someone on my team, they know I mean it, and that is far more valuable than getting people to like me by being fake. Being unapologetically myself helped me gain the trust of key partners and donors.

Once you choose how you show up, it takes work and discipline to actually do it consistently. That was a true eye-opener for me, and it took me time to find balance between showing up authentically and getting the results I wanted.

As I reflect on integrating these three prongs into my authentic leadership style, I realize that it all started with trusting in myself first. To be successful in fundraising and I would argue in business, you need to find the best person to negotiate, and it's okay if it's not you. Strategizing in the background is in line with my authentic self compared to being in the limelight with the risk of not closing the donation. The most important thing is to gain the trust of the team and work together toward celebrating successes!

Years later, the former chair of the host organization congratulated me on the success of the campaign and reminded me that I was the right person for the job. He often speaks about leadership as driving a team bus—you choose who comes on the bus *and* you are in the driver's seat. Today, he is one of my champions.

My advice to young leaders like my daughter Mia is believe in yourself, do the work, and never stop learning and challenging your belief. It might not be on your timeline. Never be afraid to ask for help when you need it. Trust in the process.

INTERIM
by Meghan Rehbein

THE COUCHES IN THE president's office were the hard, institutional kind of couches where you perched on the edge in your skirt
suit and heels because you didn't dare to get comfortable. They
weren't the kind of couches that you tucked your feet up and snug-
gled under a blanket to watch a movie. They were designed to force
formality and discomfort, in keeping with the white marble fire-
place, curated bookshelves, and carefully selected local art. When
I sat on these couches, I was on notice. I was on best behavior. I
was there to prove my value to the organization, and repeatedly
I was failing. I felt that failure keenly the day that I worked up the
courage to ask when the "interim" would be removed from my title.

This was the second time in a span of two years that I was
in an interim leadership role in the same organization. We were
weeks past the date that the president had given me originally for
when I'd be named to the permanent position. Every person I met
with asked the same question: When will they give you the job for
real? Never mind that I'd been doing the job for real for nearly six
months by that point. I'm not a person who thrives on conflict or
hard conversations, and I've had to train myself over the years to
make sure I have them when they are needed. It was clear that I

had to ask—that the president wasn't going to bring it up. I had been waiting a while, thinking that because I was getting results in turning the department around, in building back staff morale and community trust, that he'd notice, and with appreciation offer me the status and title—and salary—to go with the effort I was making. So as I sat on those hard, uncomfortable couches, with a yawning pit in my stomach, I forced myself to ask: Can we talk about my role, and the move from interim to permanent?

I didn't expect him to just give me a date. But I also didn't expect him to equivocate on his original commitment to name me permanent VP, and to say that he thought it would be best that we do a search. Looking earnest, and probably believing it himself, he explained that the university was going to post the job, and that I should apply and go through the search process so that I would be viewed as having achieved the role legitimately.

That word, *legitimately*, stuck with me for weeks after that. Was I not legitimately leading the organization already? Was I an illegitimate leader because I hadn't done the dog and pony show for the campus this time around? What about the process of going through a search would confer legitimacy? It was still just him making the decision about who to hire! And what did it say about my value—as a leader and to the organization—that my best efforts were not viewed by my boss as legitimate leadership? What did it mean that this was the second time this was happening to me in the same organization?

Two years prior, I had been in my first interim leadership role in this organization and was the candidate that was not selected for the permanent role. Following the resignation of the first VP, my colleague Jen and I were named to interim co-leadership over our department of twelve. We were friends and colleagues with complementary skill sets, peer roles, and a habit of collaborative work, so it made good sense. When the position was posted a week or two into our interim tenure, Jen and I discussed whether each of us would be interested in the role on a permanent basis. She wasn't, I was, and so I submitted my materials to the search firm as an internal candidate.

If you've ever been an internal candidate for a role—particularly one serving in the role on an interim basis—you know how hard it is to keep confidentiality. My whole office knew, the search committee knew, the president and cabinet knew. It was just a matter of time before it was common knowledge on campus. My one request to the recruiter was that if I was not truly a candidate for the role— or there were candidates that were just that much more qualified than I was—that I be offered a chance to withdraw from the search before the final round, which takes place over a span of two days and is a very public process. I didn't want to go through the stress and public humiliation of being a third-rate candidate in a public process because they thought they needed to "give me a look" as an internal candidate in an interim leadership role.

When we got to the final stages, I was one of two candidates that was invited to interview. The interview included meetings with various groups of stakeholders around campus, a public presentation on some aspect of the department's work, one-on-one interviews with the president and key cabinet members, and a cocktail party to prove that I was able to network effectively. A staff member, who had a general air of forgetfulness and clumsiness, managed to leave a copy of the other candidate's resume on my desk the day before my interview. As much as I knew I should, it was impossible for me to simply drop it into the recycling bin. I had to read it—at that point what did it matter if I knew who I was competing with for the role?

There's a moment in a situation like that where you just know. You know that you don't stack up. You know that there's no equivalency between your skills, ability, past performance, or future prospects. I was angry and embarrassed before I was even done reading the first page of his résumé. How dare the committee and the search firm put me in this position? Why didn't they tell me that the competition was so far out of my league that I was going to look ridiculous? Was I there as a counterpoint only to say, "Look what you'll get if you don't pick our guy?" What the hell was I going to do? The search committee chair reached out specifically to tell me I was not a token internal candidate, that I was not being gratuitously included at this stage of the search. But the fact that she reached out to tell me that just reinforced my sense that I was unworthy and that I looked ridiculous trying to punch above my weight.

It was too late to withdraw, although I considered it. The full-day interview was later that week, and I had to play my role in this process so that the president and university could show that they did a true search and picked the best candidate. I knew it wasn't going to be me, and it wasn't. I got to sit on those hard, uncomfortable couches to hear the bad news—they were hiring him.

"Of course you are," I said. "If I was in your position, if I was on the hiring committee, I would have hired him instead of me. There's no comparison between our experiences." This was my narrative—it felt like every single blessed member of the university community needed to talk to me about it. I couldn't let them see how embarrassed I was, how disappointed in myself, how little I valued my own potential as a leader at this point. My diminishment was compounded when the newly hired VP decided that only I was capable of managing his onboarding and introduction to the university community. I was in the attic of the building that housed our offices when I got that call, and it felt like the sloping ceiling was closing in on me. He had to know I was his only rival for the role, and how difficult and embarrassing it would be for me to take on this project. He had to know and not care.

Over the next fourteen months I came to learn that not only did he not care, but he also seemed to want that diminishment. Following his successful onboarding and introduction, he rewarded me with a demotion—being sure to let me know that it was for my own good. I was doing two jobs, and neither one of them well, he said. Pick the internal half of your job, he suggested, because he'd probably fire me if I picked the external half. I was no good at it, according to him. I accepted his judgment that I was incapable of what was needed to lead, but that I could be highly effective if I stayed behind the scenes. And over those fourteen months, I helped him execute a plan for the office that resulted in terrible staff morale, high turnover, major dips in fundraising, and a lack of trust among alumni, students, faculty, and staff. Jen left after a protracted campaign on his part, including a demotion and public humiliation whenever he had the chance. I stayed, and I still could not tell you why. I was not an official second-in-command, although I was running the operations of the department. My title had been reduced, my salary curtailed, my office location moved, and my working life made significantly harder. And still I stayed, thinking that at some point it would all be better.

The second time I was named to an interim role was much more dramatic. On Halloween of that year, I had taken a half day to go trick-or-treating with my kids. I was carrying a pillowcase full of candy in one hand, and a glass of wine in the other, talking to other moms as we walked down the sidewalk when my phone started blowing up around 4:00 p.m. from coworkers in my office building. "Why do I have to leave the building?" "What's going on?" "Is there an active shooter event?" Curious, but with absolutely no idea about what was going on, I reached out and found out that everyone on the first floor of our building had been told to leave at 4:00 p.m. and that there were police in the building. A few hours later I received a call from the president asking me to be in his office at 8:00 a.m. the next morning, and letting me know that the VP was suspended, and that the president needed me to step into an informal leadership role in the office. He'd explain it all when we met.

The couches in his office were again the setting for a pivotal conversation. I was to take on the leadership role in the office, but without even the interim title until they could work out the details of the VP's departure. He told me that I'd be given the interim title when that was done, and that they'd wait a few months for the board to settle down. I'd already been through the search; he told me he regretted not choosing me fourteen months prior. We sat in his office on the couches, and he told me that he would name me to the role permanently. March, maybe, or April, but definitely in the spring.

I was flattered—who wouldn't be—but also scared. The office I was leading was in shambles. Office politics and rivalries were sharp, and there was little sense of team between areas that had to work collaboratively. The university community had little trust in the office, and the community at large had pulled back from giving due to some very public missteps, and existential threats facing the university. I was being given a second chance to lead—but had an uphill battle and an interim title. So here I was, in early November following a disastrous few months, faced with a nearly demolished staff, processes and procedures that were in disarray, alumni that were up in arms, and faculty that didn't trust us to do anything right, being placed into the same interim leadership role I had held fifteen months earlier.

There were no goals at that point—we were holding on for dear life. Six weeks later, the president was able to name me interim VP formally. I knuckled down again, and got to work rebuilding the team internally, focusing on being transparent, and on building autonomy among staff. Some of the things that I had been complicit in over the fourteen months of the former VP's tenure needed to be brought out into the light and discussed—like the fact that we had decimated our alumni engagement efforts through a series of poor choices, and that the budget reality meant that we didn't have resources to commit to the effort of rebuilding. Other issues that resulted from decisions that were made during his tenure needed to be addressed and fixed, like lack of any major gifts in the pipeline, or a misrepresentation to a grant funder of how their gifts were used. My confidence in my own leadership grew significantly during this time. I was able to make strides in getting the office in order, rebuilding morale, gaining the trust of my team as well as faculty and staff around the university, and building relationships with community members that had previously been wary of us due to the negative press surrounding the college and our advancement operations.

The first time I served as interim leader I was performing the role—doing what I thought needed to be done to be "seen" as a leader. The second time around I was embodying the role. I was the leader. I was it, and I knew it. The doubts that plagued me when I was faced with his résumé were no longer an issue. I knew that I was better at it than he was—I had proof in every gift that rolled in, every faculty member that reached out, in every staff member that chose to stay and be present in their role.

So by the time March and April rolled around, I was confident enough to ask the president when he expected to name me to the role permanently. I still had the butterflies in my stomach that I always had when I sat on those couches in that room. But I thought I knew that I was doing the job well.

I was surprised to hear him say that while he still intended to name me permanent, he and the board felt that it was necessary to do a search so that I had legitimacy in the role. I was confident, but still trusting at that point, and took him at his word. It stung—he was telling me what an excellent job I was doing as interim—but I decided to believe that it would work out in the end. We had already discussed salary, and I knew that I'd be making about 20 percent more when I was named permanent, and I also knew the financial situation the university was in. The previous VP had been given a very generous package to leave the institution, so I figured that maybe it was a little bit of a financial decision as much as it was a referendum on my leadership ability or worth to the organization. The president shared that he had named another of my colleagues as the chair of his search committee, but that it would be a quick search, handled without a search firm, and that I could expect to be in the role formally most likely by the end of the fiscal year.

When they finally posted the position six or eight weeks later, I applied. Before this time, I had jokingly referred to the colleague that had been named as chair of the search as "the place decisions went to die" based on his habit of letting things sit on his desk until a decision was no longer necessary. I knew that the search wasn't going to progress quickly without outside influence. I waited a few weeks and asked the president for an update. He gave me the boilerplate—John is running the search; he'll be in touch soon. I started asking every week—it was the end of the fiscal year at this point, and there was no end in sight, no progress being made that I, or anyone I asked, was aware of.

After about eight weeks of this, something flipped in my head. I was having the same conversation, on the same couches, with the same man over and over again. Nothing was going to change unless I made it change. I had started to believe that little voice in my head saying, "Maybe you aren't the right person, maybe you aren't good enough for the permanent role," and I knew that way lay danger. The last time I didn't get the role, I let someone else define what I was worth. I let someone else demote and demoralize me, and I believed them. I could not let that happen again.

A position that I had interviewed for at another organization two years prior had been reposted a few months before. I reached out to the talent management lead at that organization to have a casual conversation—note my interest and see what was happening with that role. It happened to be at a sweet spot in the search—they were in the final stage of the search and one of the two candidates had withdrawn the day before. He asked if I would consider coming into the search at this late date (since I had been through the early stages of the same search two years prior) and I agreed. That was how, in just ten days from my initial outreach, I ended up with an offer of employment.

Now I had a dilemma. I hadn't expected that—at all—when I reached out about this role. I had expected to have a conversation, maybe get some insight into what my worth was in the job market at this point. When I agreed to be a finalist, I expected that participating in the search might be enough to galvanize my current organization to action—would they truly be okay losing me in this role? But I never expected to be the candidate chosen, or to get the highly attractive offer that they presented me with.

The next morning, I went to the president and shared the whole story. My frustration with the search here (which he knew), my initial outreach and the serendipitous timing of the other search, and the result—an offer of employment at another organization. His response? "Good luck with that organization, we are sorry to see you go." No counteroffer, no question about whether there were circumstances under which I would stay. Just, "Okay, goodbye." Talk about feeling deflated. Here I was with an amazing offer and all I could think about was that they didn't actually want me at the organization I had been working so hard to rebuild. They didn't value me at all.

It took a long time for me to build back and to understand that my value has nothing to do with what other people are willing to pay me, or whether they want me in a role—interim or otherwise. I learned that I am in control of determining my worth, that I can always choose differently. I've taken this approach with all the roles that I've had since my second interim experience and I'm a better person, and a better leader, because of it.

P.S. Recently I took on an interim role for the third time in my career, this time in a very different organization. I took this third interim role knowing that I was interested in the permanent position and also that I did not fit the traditional candidate profile. Over the course of about nine months, I had the opportunity to embody the leadership role again—this time with a much more satisfying outcome!

∽ MEET THE AUTHORS ∽

ONOME AKO

Onome Ako, CEO of Action Against Hunger Canada, is a trail-blazing leader in the global fight against hunger and malnutrition. Her career is distinguished by a deep commitment to community-led solutions for ensuring the fundamental human right to food. Onome's impactful work spans over 20 countries, where she has collaborated with prestigious organizations like Amref Health Africa and World Vision Canada.

Educationally, she holds a BA in English from Obafemi Awolowo University, Nigeria, an MA in International Affairs and Diplomacy from Ahmadu Bello University, Nigeria, and an MSc in Management of NGOs and Social Policy from the London School of Economics. As chair of the Board of Directors of the Canadian Partnership for Women and Children's Health (CanWaCH) and a member of the Centennial College International Development program's advisory committee, Onome exemplifies leadership that transcends borders.

Her recognition as one of 2021 Canada's Most Powerful Women and the recipient of World Vision Canada's "Voice of the Children" Award in 2022, and winner of the RBC Women of Influence social change award underscores her influence and authority.

DELPHINE HASLÉ

Delphine Haslé is an esteemed executive in the charitable sector, distinguished by her Certified Fundraising Executive (CFRE) accreditation and fluency in two languages. Her professional journey is marked by a high degree of motivation and skill in developing philanthropic strategies, ranging from annual programs to capital campaigns. Delphine's extensive experience in operational and financial management is evidenced through her adeptness in C-suite and boardroom settings.

A consummate fundraiser, Delphine excels as a bridge between donors and institutions, finding her greatest inspiration in this vital connection. Known for her warmth, excellent communication skills, transparency, and passion, she is highly regarded by donors and colleagues alike.

§

MEGHAN REHBEIN, EDD

Dr. Meghan Rehbein serves with distinction as the eleventh Dean of Douglass, a position she has held since July 2022. Her journey with Douglass began in 2018, initially as Associate Dean for Strategic Initiatives, where she focused on fostering collaborative opportunities, particularly in communications and sustainability. Prior to her current role, Meghan played a pivotal role in successfully concluding the Power of 100 Years Campaign for Douglass and has served as Vice President for Institutional Advancement at Georgian Court University.

Her academic credentials are impressive, holding a bachelor's degree from Hampshire College, a master's degree from Sacred Heart University, and an EdD from Stockton University. With over two decades of experience in nonprofit leadership, higher education, and health and human services organizations, Meghan brings a wealth of knowledge and expertise. Her research delves into the intersection of gender and leadership development in the nonprofit sector.

Listen to the podcast episode!

REFLECTION QUESTIONS

1. The term "impostor syndrome" describes the feeling of "not enoughness" experienced by women leaders. Have you ever experienced this feeling?

2. In Onome's story, she repeatedly describes being boxed in by assumptions people make about her. Can you think of a time in your life when people made assumptions about you and your work? What were those assumptions?

3. Being an internal candidate for a leadership position is a great example of overcoming a perception barrier. How would you approach this process as an aspiring leader? What pitfalls could you anticipate? If you were on the hiring committee, what would you be looking for from an internal candidate that would set them apart from the others?

4. In her story, Delphine speaks at length about the importance of trust. What is your definition of trust? Can you give an example from your own experiences?

5. Meghan explains in the conclusion of her story that she is always in control of determining her worth. She can always choose differently. What do you think would be the challenges for you to step up and value your contribution every day at work? Can you unequivocally say that you determine your own worth? Is it a work in progress? (There's no right or wrong answer here . . . just reflection.)

6. If there was *one* thing you'd like to change about the way people see you at your office, what would it be?

EMBODIED ROLES

The CEO's personal leadership identity sets the mood for the organization. The more the CEO's identity aligns with the social identity of the group, the more influence they will have. The challenge is that this kind of relationship also creates a feeling of being "always on," blurring the lines between personal and professional identities. This fact also has health implications for leaders.

DIGNITY
by Justine Hendricks

Dig·ni·ty: the state or quality of being worthy of honor or respect.
"a man of dignity and unbending principle"

SEPTEMBER 1978: I was five years old and ready to go to school. I was thrilled for the opportunity to meet new friends, learn in a different environment, and to take on the world. My mom loved to tell me that when I was born, I almost jumped out of her womb. The doctor had said it was because I was so ready for the world. For me, this was chapter two: entering the school environment.

I was so excited that I had carefully researched the name of my school and where it was located. I had a uniform that I was proud to wear and could not wait until I could meet my fellow students. On the first day of school, my mom brought me to the corner and we waited for my new chapter to begin. And just like the doctor said, I jumped onto the bus as soon as it stopped in front of me. I hopped in and sat down near the front.

I ended up arriving late to school that first day because the bus driver had missed my stop. By the time I reached school, class had already begun. In fact, the school had already called home to report my absence. Now that I have three girls of my own, I can only imagine how scary that call would have been for my parents. Thankfully, the stress was short-lived as I arrived on campus shortly after. I was ready to start my new chapter. I remember arriving at school, holding my bag just like I had seen my mom hold her briefcase. As I walked up to the school, I was quickly approached by a nun. She seemed very happy to see me (I'm guessing she was also incredibly relieved that the missing student on the first day of school had been found). Before she could even get a word out, I looked at her and said, "Good morning! My name is Justine Hendricks, and I am here to go to school!" I'll never forget her warm smile. We both knew I was in the right place.

My kind greeter escorted me to my kindergarten class. I was expecting to be placed in a class full of students, but my classroom was empty. My classmates were on their first break, so I patiently waited for their return. What an unorthodox first day of school, huh?

I didn't realize this at the time, but this wasn't just a first for me—I was also a first for the school. Maybe it was because I was so focused on the strange way to start the day, but I did not notice that out of all of my classmates, I was the only kid that was of a visible minority. In fact, I was one of the first students of a visible minority that the school had ever had. Today I am thankful that my parents did not say anything about it. I was so proud of my school, my uniform, and the opportunity to meet new friends that on this crucial, formative day of my life I never once felt like I was different because I was treated like everyone else: a young student with an opportunity to learn. Equally.

I remember coming home and sharing my new adventures over dinner. My parents would chime in to both share in my excitement and underscore some important lessons that have served me to this day:

- Never judge a book by its cover.
- Life isn't always fair and it is our job to call it out.
- There is always context . . . and we don't always know what the context is (or have context to understand everything).

Twelve years later, I graduated from Villa Sainte-Marcelline or as we called it, "La Villa." When I reflect on my time there, I am thankful for the lessons above, and all the friendships that were established.

I attended my twenty-five-year high school reunion a few years ago. It was such a meaningful opportunity to reconnect, remember the past, and celebrate what we had all become. During the reunion, one of my classmates shared their perspective about my arrival at school in 1978. I found out that there was a much bigger context for my arrival at La Villa than I knew about.

What I didn't know of, as a proud new student that was ready to take on a new chapter, was that some of the parents saw my arrival at the school as a problem. It was enough of a problem that it warranted a formal request to have me—a five-year-old little girl that was so proud of the uniform that granted her the opportunity to be like every other kid—removed from the school because "a black five-year-old girl" did not belong.

You already know that I graduated from this school. The request was (thankfully) denied.

My parents never said a word about any of this to me. They understood the importance of protecting my dignity. And in 1978,

La Villa also understood how a decision to lean into equality could safeguard a little girl's confidence and preserve her drive to make a meaningful impact in the world. On that day, forty-four years ago, I was given an equal opportunity to learn like any other child—an inflection point that determined the trajectory of my potential. Today, I am the president and CEO of an organization with 2,300 employees that serves over 100,000 customers and a $47 billion portfolio. This future was made possible because my school, my parents, and my classmates protected my dignity. Whenever I am called to stay true to my beliefs and values, I understand that I am simply paying forward the opportunity for another child, schoolbag in hand, to take on their next chapter with dignity as their superpower.

Aristotle said, "Dignity does not consist in possessing honors, but in the consciousness that we deserve them." Nobody starts out as a CEO, and everybody starts somewhere. My career path started in 2004 at a bank. My dream was to be an architect, but because I graduated during a recession, I opted to have some independence by getting myself a job first. I was also very eager to get going and start working. Suddenly, I had business cards with my name on them, and I was working for a financial institution. I credit a lot of my management philosophy to these ten years of experience. To this day I:

- Hold a profound love and respect for the customer.
- Understand the importance of high standards and ethics, especially when you're growing.
- Value exceptional customer service.
- Focus on making a difference every day through my individual actions.

- Hold a healthy respect for the complexity of change within organizations.
- Strive to make every employee feel valued, no matter the size and scale of the organization.
- Leverage curiosity as a powerful tool to learn, solve problems, and seize future opportunities.

There was an expression at the bank—and I believe this holds true today—that the key to your career path is to look for opportunities to manage people. It was an unspoken rule that if you wanted to progress in your career, you had to learn how to be an effective leader. I understood right away that an impactful leader would contribute or detract from your employee experience which would, in turn, directly influence your customer satisfaction.

It's important to recognize that in the '90s, the employee value proposition and sense of purpose largely focused on profitability. The race to showcase your value was solely focused on how much money you could make for the organization. And in some respects, this meant that the employee experience suffered.

I saw this firsthand when I was working in Ottawa. I was progressing through the management ranks and was approached to transfer from a unit in the west end to a downtown location. The potential career shift meant that I would be working for a new regional VP. Before deciding to apply, I asked to meet the new leader. I still recall meeting this person for the first time. After thanking her for the chance to meet, I remember her saying, "Everyone tells me how great you are, but I needed to see it for myself." I wasn't expecting this, but I took this opportunity to prove my value.

"If I am the successful candidate, what is one thing you would like to be different in thirty days?" I asked.

She replied, "Get my phone to stop ringing!"

Without really understanding the request, I assured her that I could get it done and I got the job. I was feeling confident because this was a return to the unit that I began my career in. There were some familiar faces, and some new team members that I was eager to work with.

On my first day in the downtown office, I was still pondering what she meant by "get my phone to stop ringing." Within four hours of my arrival, it became pretty clear what she meant. Because there was an obvious lack of leadership and support for the staff, anytime there was a customer question or complaint, the employees were handing out the regional VP's business card. Then her phone would start ringing with a multitude of problems from the field. Employees were not empowered to make decisions, and they felt powerless to offer any solution on their own. The result? They defaulted to pushing every interaction to the top in order to find some sort of resolution for their customers.

The chaos seeped into the employee experience too. At one point, a staff member lashed out because she was so upset with how disorganized the backroom was where we stored banking machines and branch supplies. This staff member had taken a marker and left a sternly worded message to everyone about the mess. As a young manager, I was disappointed that this employee felt the appropriate solution was to destroy bank property. And even more ironically, that the message was about telling the coworkers to be respectful of the workspace.

It did not take me long to find out who had written the "marker message," but instead of jumping into action, I decided to go home that evening and think of the best way to approach this situation. I came into work the next day prepared to discipline her and integrate her response into her year-end review. I was equipped with clear expectations for how to behave in the workplace and rehearsed language to let her know that this behavior would not be tolerated. I was ready. Or at least I thought I was.

She came into my office, and I started with a question I had strategically prepared: "Help me understand what pushed you to ruin bank property in order to communicate with your team?"

She replied, "When you have tried every possible way to gain someone's attention, when you've been consistently ignored by your colleagues, when you've run out of ways to bring up the challenge, and when you must take time out of your time off and stay past closing hours to ensure you'll have clear access to your work area the following day—well, you get to the point where there is nothing left. Not even your dignity."

She had a point.

Every day had become a fight for survival in this unit. In the absence of effective communication, the staff had set their own rules of the jungle and the lack of leadership had validated it. This was such an important moment in my leadership journey, one where you truly empathize and walk in someone else's shoes. We spend more time at work than we do at home, and a toxic environment has the power to deteriorate one's basic identity, especially if they are powerless to provide feedback.

I went into this interaction expecting to reprimand an employee that was out of line and instead, I found myself apologizing. I vowed to her that I would ensure she would never have to feel like this again, that her feedback and request for support was always valid, and that ensuring her working environment was respected would be a basic, standardized commitment from the bank. She thanked me and I stayed in my office to reflect on an important lesson that would stay with me forever.

In addition to learning that every situation must be approached with an open mind and authentic curiosity, I learned that an employee's dignity must be protected at all costs. Until then, I had never seen how a negative working environment could impact a person over time. Left unresolved, a toxic workplace can bring about uncharacteristically negative behaviors from employees that would be easy to judge without the full context of the situation. It became clear to me that my job as a leader was to protect my employee's dignity. And the way to do that was not to reprimand, but to remove roadblocks. As a leader, it's crucial to understand that long-term satisfaction is the cumulation of all of your short-term actions. Each and every day, it's important to remain calm, composed, attentive, and focused on the small actions that will help build self-respect and confidence. At the root of empowerment, you will find dignity.

Fast Forward to Today, 2023

Today, I am a single mom of three beautiful daughters that I raised mostly on my own, with the support of an amazing village of friends and family. When I was approached to put my name forward for a new role, I knew that these kinds of opportunities to lead do not come often, and that they don't come to everyone. I made a promise to myself during the interview process: no matter how attractive, desirable, or eager I was for the role, I would earn it by honoring the values that I have learned. This way I would always stay true to who I am. I committed to sharing my true thoughts with the recruitment panel, answering questions during the process with honesty and in support of my values.

I got the job. I am a new CEO faced with the opportunity of a lifetime: to make a huge difference in an industry that feeds the world. As president and CEO of Farm Credit Canada, I now have the opportunity to set the tone, lead the way, and leverage these lessons that I have learned to make a difference in the lives of people, an industry, and the world.

When I stepped into this new adventure, I had the gift of fresh eyes and perspective. I began to see that dignity is multidimensional: it is felt in the way that I approach my team, my employees, my customers, and stakeholders. Dignity is embedded in my mindset and attitude and it sets the tone for every interaction from the top of the organization downward.

As the leader, it is my responsibility to uphold the dignity of those around me. Dignity creates an environment where people feel valued, respected, and as a result, they feel more engaged; this puts their minds at ease, it unleashes their curiosity, it ignites their drive, and we as a team achieve tremendous impact as a result.

To make this happen you must uphold the dignity of everyone: the grocery store worker, the parking lot attendant, the bus driver, the foreign worker in the field, the dry-cleaning staff. By now it should be clear to you: you cannot pick and choose when you turn it on or off. You either live with dignity and respect for others or you don't. *Period.*

What will my next chapter bring? I am confident that I will make a difference in the lives of the people in my world. I will strive to be curious, to not judge a book by its cover, and to preserve the dignity of everyone I meet. Just like my birth into the world, just like my first day of school, and just like my enthusiasm for this new chapter as CEO, I am confident that I have the ability to motivate those around me. Dignity, respect, and empowerment—that's what keeps me energized and moving forward as a leader.

THE SYSTEM
by Janet Donovan

Norfolk Naval Base, Norfolk, Virginia, 10:00 a.m., December 23

Captain Donovan, Counsel for the Respondent: Good morning, board members. I am Captain Janet Donovan, Judge Advocate General's Corps, U. S. Navy, here as Counsel for the Respondent representing Commander James Lewis*.

I come before you today to request an extension. As you know, I was just given notice of the date of this hearing last Thursday, December nineteenth, just four days ago. The regulations require a minimum of thirty days' notice. As you will see, the prison warden has given permission for my client to attend this hearing, as is his right, but the warden requires time to arrange for interstate transfer.

Furthermore, with such short notice and given the fact that today is December twenty-third, it has been impossible for our witnesses to obtain flights during the Christmas holidays to attend today's hearing. I respectfully request a continuance until January twenty-first to allow Commander Lewis to be present, and to provide time for witnesses to arrange for flights to attend the hearing.

Board President: Denied. Government, are you ready to proceed?

Counsel for the Government: We are.

Board President: Please begin.

Captain Donovan: Mr. President, if I may, Commander Lewis has a right to be present for the hearing. Our request for in-person presence has been denied. Our previous request to the Government for Commander Lewis to appear via video teleconference has been denied. Our previous request for Commander Lewis to appear by phone has been denied. My request for funding to travel to meet with my client in person in advance of the hearing has been denied. We are not prepared to proceed today. Additionally, as a personal matter, my daughter is scheduled for surgery this afternoon, and I must take her and be present.

Board President: Captain Donovan, we are proceeding with the hearing and will be finished today. Government, is there speakerphone capability in this conference room?

Counsel for the Government: Sir, we could do that. Yes, sir.

Board President: Captain Donovan, is Commander Lewis available by phone right now?

Captain Donovan: Yes, sir. He is.

Board President: We will take a fifteen-minute recess for the Government to get Commander Lewis on the line. Counselor, we are proceeding with or without you. I suggest you make other arrangements for your daughter.

§

Decades Earlier

It's Friday of the first week of law school. I've survived. The Socratic method whereby professors randomly call on students to brief a case and ask questions was, in fact, as intimidating as advertised. My classmates are wicked smart. I've met a dozen or so people in our small groups where we will learn legal research and writing, and I've met the people who sit to my left and right in class. And now, I'm headed to the first-year student reception complete with awkward unstructured intros. At times like this, I wish I liked beer—that equalizing beverage that says, "I'm approachable."

The social equivalent of bumper cars begins: "I'm Janet. Nice to meet you."

"Where did you go to undergrad?"

"What made you decide to become a lawyer?"

"What section are you in? Where are you from? Where are you living? What kind of law do you want to practice?"

People chat while simultaneously looking over your shoulder to see whether there's someone else they see that makes them think they should move on from you to the next person.

Honestly, I don't remember what I said during these conversations: Undergrad? College of Wooster. From? Lakewood, Ohio. Why law school? Something akin to Superman's "Truth, Justice, and the American Way," which I undoubtedly said with all the naïveté of someone who'd just finished her first week of law school.

I play social bumper cars, too, until I meet colleague number six who says: "I'm in law school to figure out how to smuggle drugs into the country from South America and not go to jail." I laugh a nervous laugh. He takes a sip of his beer, elaborates slightly, and moves on to the next person.

Surely, he must be messing with me. . . . Nope, I don't think so. This colleague number six came to law school to become a modern-day consiglieri. I left—nauseous and reeling at the thought that someone in our class might have goals to use this education to pervert the system for his own illicit purposes.

By Monday morning's crim law class, I'd fully compartmentalized this two-minute interlude with colleague number six and suppressed my initial conclusion. Not possible. My vision of Superman's unfurled cape returned.

Professors grilled us—randomly calling on us to brief a case with the facts, the issue, and majority and minority opinions. What did the precedents say? How could the case be differentiated from others? Every class reinforced my previously held beliefs that the law was an honorable profession, that our system appropriately placed the burden of proof on the government, and that, although imperfect, it worked. I envisioned myself joining this great profession and hoped to be worthy of becoming a member of the bar someday.

Through the cases in our textbooks, I learned of the burden on attorneys as officers of the court to serve the law as something greater than ourselves, and that those who failed to do so were disciplined and disbarred. I saw my classmates studying in library carrels till midnight closing. In an era of dial-up, pay-by-the-minute internet, access to legal cases was limited to those with the speed and skills to find them hiding among the serpentine library stacks.

Tension was palpable but without the rumored cutthroat antics where key cases were competitively razor-bladed and removed from law reporters to prevent others from finding the answers.

The next three years passed like the Blue Streak roller coaster ride at my childhood Cedar Point amusement park; the ride was short but each twist and turn was a white-knuckle moment. Fast forward to the November after law school graduation, after passing the bar exam, when I donned my new attorney's suit of armor, still attempting to find that cross between a power look that spelled confidence and a feminine look that took the edge off a bulldog. With a sense of pride and butterflies in my stomach, I stood, raised my right hand in a room full of hundreds of others, and swore before the Supreme Court of the State of Ohio as follows:

"In my capacity as an attorney and officer of the Court, I will conduct myself with dignity and civility and show respect toward judges, court staff, clients, fellow professionals, and all other persons. I will honestly, faithfully, and competently discharge the duties of an attorney at law."

I'd done it, and with a celebratory microwave oven from my parents for my bare-bones apartment, my legal career was about to begin. Justice—justice you shall pursue.

While in law school, I had no idea what type of law I wanted to practice. I wasn't particularly interested in criminal law, remembering that my father served as a court-appointed attorney in one criminal case and vowed never to handle another because mistakes made when losing people's money are nothing compared to mistakes made when loss of liberty hangs in the balance.

Nonetheless, the thought of being in the criminal courtroom was intriguing. I'd done well in trial tactics (right up until I argued in my mock closing argument that the babysitter in the case took better care of the children than the mother. Fairly obvious trial tactics tip: never glorify a babysitter over a mother).

As I considered my options, the military came to visit my law school. The Judge Advocate General's (JAG) Corps. Yes, the United States military—the JAG Corps—specifically the Navy JAG Corps. Even its insignia depicted Truth, Justice, and the American Way. The mill rinde, an ancient French symbol of equal justice for all under the law, nestled between two oak leaves, represented the honor, courage, and commitment required of uniformed Navy JAG Corps attorneys, who served both the prosecution and the defense by making their best arguments from which the truth would emerge. I became increasingly invested in the idea of serving my country in uniform for a cause greater than myself, and I set my sights on joining the Navy JAG Corps.

With the help of many, in a small courtroom in Seattle, Washington, my father-in-law, a captain in the United States Navy, commissioned me as an officer by asking me to repeat these words: "I, Janet Donovan, having been appointed an officer in the United States Navy, do solemnly swear (or affirm) that I will support and defend the Constitution of the United States against all enemies, foreign or domestic; that I will bear true faith and allegiance to the same; that I take this obligation freely, without any mental reservation or purpose of evasion; and that I will well and faithfully discharge the duties of the office on which I am about to enter; So help me God."

With these words, I joined a worldwide law firm of 1,200 uniformed attorneys serving a Navy of almost six hundred ships and saw myself as part of a cohesive judicial system that valued effort, attention to detail, and collegiality. As promised, I had my own caseload. As a newly commissioned judge advocate, I had much to learn. Being in hearings and trials during the day left little time for the level of prep required of a novice, and the hours were long. But as we churned through cases, I saw justice being meted out appropriately. From my seat, military justice in action lived up to my every expectation. I felt somehow like I was standing on high moral ground when I worked my cases. I worked with defense counsel and commands to ensure cases were being handled at the proper levels of discipline. I watched military commanders and military judges weigh extenuating and mitigating circumstances and grant leniency where it was warranted, yet with an awareness that disproportionately light sentences could have a ripple effect on military good order and discipline. And in those cases where I judged that a rare acquittal should have resulted in a conviction, I took solace in the fact that the bedrock of our system is that a guilty person should go free before an innocent should be wrongly convicted.

I felt tremendous pride in being part of a judicial system where prosecutors litigate aggressively, defense counsel defend zealously, and command attorneys advise military commanders about judicial and nonjudicial options for infractions of the Uniform Code of Military Justice and are influential in those decisions, helping to ensure that only those cases that warrant court-martial receive court-martial.

The first test of my belief in the system was personal and came with lightning speed. My first assignment as a Navy judge advocate: represent Marines and sailors being discharged through the disability system:

Day 1—Monday: Get an introduction to the department. Feeling welcome and confident. The other attorneys are knowledgeable and appear invested in my success.

Day 2—Tuesday: Introduction to the disability system and the range of medical conditions that drive disability determinations. Feeling overwhelmed. I don't have a medical background. How will I accurately assess the options my clients have and advise them of the risks of appearing before the administrative panel that could conclude they should receive fewer benefits than they've already been offered?

Day 3—Wednesday: Watch a hearing. Feeling reassured. Each of the senior officers serving as hearing officers on the panel is well prepared, and personally and professionally determined to ensure the right outcome. They will not let me fail. A senior Marine Colonel, a senior Navy Captain, and a senior medical officer, it's clear they believe the futures of these servicemembers lie in their hands, not mine. Whew!

Days 4 and 5—Thursday and Friday: Review my assigned cases for the following week and prepare.

Day 6—Monday: Meet my first client among many stacked like cordwood in a waiting room full of clients. Thirty minutes later, walk him into a hearing that would determine his military future. Whether he would be in or out of the military, and, if out, with a disability rating from 0 to 100 percent.

Days 7–91: Dive daily into the next batch of client military medical records, medical research, and disability cases. Watch and learn from the panel in every hearing.

Day 92: Review the file of Corporal Jameson* in preparation for his hearing the following Monday. Nothing particularly challenging about his case jumps out at me.

Monday morning comes. As Corporal Jameson and others wait in the waiting room, I meet with my first client who awkwardly asks me about where he might go on Rush Street in Chicago, an area known for its wild nightlife, suggesting he likes to party. I ignore him. We finish his hearing, and he presses me again about partying downtown as we wrap up. I dismiss him with some advice to ask his fellow Marines since I've never been to Rush Street.

Before I could meet with my next client, I am summoned upstairs to the boss's office for a one-way conversation while standing at attention. My superior's sentence starts with "Lieutenant Donovan, you have the right to remain silent— anything you say can and will be used against you in a court of law . . ."

I have been accused of an offense. I am in a daze. Who? What? Corporal Jameson? The young, enlisted Marine I haven't even met yet who is downstairs in the waiting room? That Corporal Jameson? My client? He said what? That I was sleeping with him? That we'd spent last Saturday partying downtown Chicago on Rush Street, and that we went to a hotel together?   And he described me? How? I had represented other Marines from his unit so I guess they would be able to describe me as he did. Glasses, long brown hair.

For more than a hot second, I envisioned my career, not even out of the starting blocks yet, being flushed down the drain. I could feel my knees wobble and my palms sweat. There was a twenty-pound steel plate pressing on my chest as I continued to process what was happening. I wasn't sleeping with this Marine, and I'd not even met him in person. For context, in the military, it's not just bad judgment to sleep with a client; it's a crime. For the first time, I stood in the shoes of those who are falsely accused, my world spinning, as I contemplated what might happen next.

The Uniform Code of Military Justice was chock full of possible charges: adultery (yes, adultery), conduct unbecoming an officer, and fraternization, all of which carried maximum sentences that authorized jail time, to say nothing of the potential loss of my still freshly minted law license if I were convicted. The investigating officer interviewed potential witnesses, including other Marines, and he also interviewed my husband, who answered probing questions about the state of our marriage. After several stressful days, the investigating officer recommended the allegations be dismissed. Relief!

In many ways, this experience—while harrowing—reinforced two already-held, competing maxims for me: first, exercise great professional care because anyone can allege anything; and second, the system will ultimately protect us. Whether that was a senior administrative panel determining disability ratings or an investigating officer assessing witness credibility and recommending to dismiss charges, the system would protect us all. It has protected my clients. It has protected me.

What was lost on me was that any of those witnesses could have refused to "get involved," or that the investigating officer could have said, "These are facts for a jury to decide," and recommended a trial. What was lost on me at the time was how much the system depends on the integrity and moral courage of individuals within that system. I didn't process yet that there are those whose purpose is to circumvent the system for their own gain; that there are those whose egos thrive on the power entrusted to them and act with complete disregard for the guardrails; that there are those whose cowardice in the face of adversity drives them to duck personal consequences of difficult or unpopular decisions. I didn't understand until much later that we each are "the system."

§

Returning to the Unfolding Courtroom Hearing on the Day before Christmas Eve

No extension. A fifteen-minute recess! I was fuming, and getting emotional, which is what I often do when I'm fuming. I hate that about myself.

But this was ridiculous. Where was compliance with the regulations set forth by the Secretary of the Navy? Where was the basic due process? Where were my fellow judge advocates to assist these non-lawyer board members in understanding that four days' notice the week before Christmas was not only a violation of the regulations but also unjust? Disoriented and caught completely off guard, somehow, I didn't see this coming. With more than two decades of experience, I prided myself on being able to see the playing field well and assess the range of outcomes in every case. Yet, here we were. I fumbled for my words, and I could hear my voice cracking as I tried to maintain my composure on the record. At that moment, I was glad Commander Lewis was on the phone and could only hear, but not see, the wind being knocked out of me. But why was this bothering me so?

Let me set the record straight: Commander Lewis wasn't a typical defense client. From the beginning, there was something unsettling about his case. He had already served seventeen years of combined active and reserve duty in the Navy when the case was assigned. He was an aviator, a Navy pilot, and one with significant combat experience. His military record was a highlight reel of best-of-the-best accolades. Best junior officer. Best aviator in the squadron. Number one pilot. Number one leader. A future admiral. A review of his file revealed eye-watering verbiage in every personnel evaluation throughout his active-duty career. Glowing doesn't begin to describe what they said about his aviation prowess, his leadership, and his integrity. So in my first telephone call with him, I had to ask, "Why did you leave such a promising active-duty career?"

The answer: "My mom was dying. I needed to go home to take care of her." At the end of the day, as much as he loved flying and loved serving his country in uniform, he loved his mother more, and he wasn't going to let her die alone.

Respect.

So what happened? After her passing, a colleague approached Commander Lewis about running for public office. His military record and continued service in the Navy Reserve made him an ideal candidate to unseat an incumbent from the opposite political party. Initially reluctant, he agreed. Once committed, as with everything, he gave it 100 percent, including putting every penny of his own money into this campaign. And he got close to winning. So close. Too close.

Along the way, he made a mistake that cost him dearly. He withdrew money from his campaign fund for personal use. Even if it was money he himself donated, that's illegal. And it's still illegal even though he simply faxed a copy of the check to prove he had the money, but never cashed the check, and even though he returned the money to the bank forty-five minutes later. It was a crime—one for which he now had a federal conviction and was serving eighteen months.

As I read the transcript in the file from his guilty plea, I had no doubt in my mind that the charges against Commander Lewis were political. Wire fraud—seemingly every federal prosecutor's default when they don't have anything else they can actually prove. Commander Lewis pled guilty to wire fraud. They came after him when he got too close to winning.

And now the Navy was coming, intending to characterize his military service as not honorable and to strip him of veteran's benefits. And that's why this felt so wrong to me. I judged his civilian sentence as being disproportionate to the crime, and now the Navy wanted to eviscerate his combat record too. Anything other than an honorable discharge would leave Commander Lewis with no veteran's benefits for life.

Counsel for the Government: Mr. President, the Government rests. We ask this board to discharge Commander Lewis with an other-than-honorable discharge.

Board President: We've heard from the Government. Please proceed, Counselor.

Captain Donovan: Mr. President. I renew my request for an extension. Further, I would like to consult with my client about the evidence presented by the Government before we begin and would ask for the room.

Board President: Anything you would like to ask your client you may do while we are in the room.

Captain Donovan: Sir, these are attorney-client privileged conversations that require privacy and are critical to our next steps in this hearing. Are you saying I may not consult privately with my client?

Board President: I repeat. Anything you need to discuss with your client you may do while we are in the room.

Captain Donovan: Mr. President, if you are denying my client's right to consult with his attorney, I would like to place on the record the questions I would have asked him during our consultation. Commander Lewis, please do not respond.

Board President: We will take a fifteen-minute recess to consult with the attorney for the board, and to allow you to consult with your client. Government, please stop the recording during our recess. We WILL resume in fifteen minutes.

In those fifteen minutes, Commander Lewis, his wife, and I did our best to bring character witnesses to the hearing—active and reserve officers with whom Commander Lewis had worked and flown. The first witness was there within fifteen minutes. And like something out of the movie *It's a Wonderful Life*, when the word went out that Jimmy Stewart's character, George Bailey, was in trouble and needed help, the whole world showed up. Instead of dollar bills to help George Bailey, these officers came to bring testimony—instances of character and integrity and a resolve to serve with Commander Lewis anywhere notwithstanding his conviction.

Board President: The hearing is back in session. Let's proceed. Call your first witness.

~After the first character witness.~

Counsel for the Government: Mr. President, the Government will stipulate that these additional witnesses Captain Donovan proposes to bring to the stand will all testify Commander Lewis was an excellent pilot, that they would serve with him anywhere, and that if he cannot remain in the Navy Reserve, he should receive an honorable discharge.

Board President: Captain Donovan, will the other witnesses you intend to call testify as the Government has indicated?

Captain Donovan: Yes, sir.

Board President: Then I see no need to listen to each of these witnesses. Given that the Government is willing to stipulate to their testimony, the board will consider that every witness would so testify. Captain Donovan, do you have any additional evidence to present?

Captain Donovan: Mr. President, these witnesses have dropped everything to come to this hearing with no notice and are waiting outside. I would ask the panel to hear this additional testimony.

Board President: ONE witness. Then we will close to deliberate.

The hearing proceeded to a flaming finale with an other-than-honorable discharge recommendation from the board. Not good. Not the outcome we wanted.

There is a postscript to this story. I located a loophole in the system that could work in Commander Lewis's favor. To access it, he had to find a way to remain in the Navy Reserve through-out his prison term. If he could do this, he would accumulate time toward his retirement eligibility. How could he do this? Regularly, I would download from the website, print, and mail correspon-dence courses to him in prison. I was laser-focused on these small actions. Each course mailed from the post office gave me great satisfaction that, once completed, Commander Lewis would be that much closer to some level of justice. The day his years of service crossed the twenty-year mark, I held my breath. Had I missed something, or would this cement his retirement eligibility? Ultimately, after three years of waiting on appeal, the Secretary of the Navy sent a one-page letter. There would be no new hearing, no recognition that this panel had trampled on his rights, but on his sixtieth birthday, Commander Lewis would receive the first of a lifetime of monthly retirement checks for having completed twenty years of naval service. This was not the victory I'd hoped for, but it was a victory nonetheless.

Could we have continued to rail against the storm? Probably. Were the interests of justice served? Probably not. Were the interests of the Navy served? Probably not. Did the actions of those empowered to execute justice on behalf of the Navy negatively impact the perception of fairness and belief in the system for those who participated and learned of it? Absolutely—especially for all the service members whose only experience with the system was this hearing.

I think of Tom Cruise, from the movie *A Few Good Men*, cavalierly negotiating with the prosecutor on behalf of his client while at batting practice. The baseball field, and the cryptic, flippant plea bargaining were so Hollywood as Tom Cruise negotiated on behalf of his client who smoked oregano, not marijuana. In some ways, it is how the justice system truly works. The prosecutor ensures that the interests of justice are served both by ensuring the appropriate charges and the level of punishment for the offense. This ensures consistency in the way each case is handled.

I thought I was Tom Cruise. I believed I could help the government see that stripping a decorated combat service member of his honorable discharge served no purpose. I believed I could make them see that at every step they were undermining the confidence of other decorated combat service members who were disgusted with how this was unfolding. Although those on the sidelines may not have known the law, they fundamentally understood that this was not justice; not letting Commander Lewis appear in person or by video at the hearing that would determine his fate, holding the hearing with four days' notice, coming after him for a crime unrelated to his military record all felt like an abuse of power. To them, and to me, this was such an aberration. In Hollywood, Tom Cruise would likely have pulled his JAG Corps mill rinde from his collar and slammed it on the desk of the Secretary of the Navy, demanding action against the government attorneys involved and advising that he could no longer serve in a Navy that tolerated this level of injustice.

But this is not Hollywood. Real life doesn't always come together so neatly. What was lost on me years earlier was now clear: the system only works when every member has integrity and exercises moral courage, especially those who wield the greatest positions of power. We are each the system. I learned that people are always watching, and I can shape their view of what justice looks like by the ways in which I play my role as one with positional power, as one creating the rules, as one falsely accused, as one charged with upholding the system, as one who must elevate those who come after me in the system, as one who *is* the system.

Thousands of days have passed since these events. I continued to rise through the ranks of the Navy, becoming a two-star admiral before I transitioned to my current role as president and chief executive officer for Girl Scouts in the Heart of Pennsylvania. Yet the lessons I learned during those workdays remain, and they are universal. Colleague number six exists beyond law school, and those who strive to understand the system solely for the purpose of twisting it to their personal benefit are found in every profession. There are those who—when given power—will wield it to shape the outcome they desire simply because they have the power to do so. From the largest corporations, universities, and government agencies to the smallest nonprofits and businesses, we must each learn to navigate the systems we are in, take ownership of our role in it, and see ourselves as critical to its success no matter our title or position.

To some, my transition from military lawyer to Girl Scout Council executive might seem a non sequitur. To the contrary, the opportunity to take the lessons learned in one large, bureaucratic organization steeped in history and tradition and then influence another with a proven track record of building girl leaders and over fifty million alumni was precisely the next step.

I lead now with more compassion. I have the insight and knowledge born of experience, that not everyone believes there is an individual responsibility to the system. I like to think I empower those around me to challenge the assumptions being made and to lead with integrity. I take more responsibility for ensuring processes and procedures are in place to protect everyone. Most importantly, as one of 111 Girl Scout Council CEOs at the helm of this girl leadership development organization, these lessons are critical to embed here—in girls—in ways that empower them so they have the courage, confidence, and character to take action. In these small ways, I believe I am instilling in each of us a core belief that "I am the system."

*Certain information has been anonymized to protect these clients.

⚬ MEET THE AUTHORS ⚬

JUSTINE HENDRICKS

Justine Hendricks, President and Chief Executive Officer of Farm Credit Canada (FCC), brings a wealth of experience and strategic insight to her role. Prior to joining FCC, Justine spent 17 years with Export Development Canada (EDC) and seven years with the Royal Bank of Canada, honing her expertise in financial services, organizational transformation, risk management, and the development of innovative financial products.

Justine's career has been dedicated to supporting Canadian businesses, especially in the agriculture and agri-food sectors. In 2021, she made history as EDC's first Chief Corporate Sustainability Officer, championing environmental, social, and governance principles and integrating sustainable business practices into every line of business at EDC.

Justine holds an MBA from the University of Ottawa, a Bachelor of Arts in Urban Studies from Carleton University, and a Certified Financial Planner designation. She passionately supports youth innovation and leadership as a member and chair of the Digital Opportunity Trust and has held significant roles with the Forum for Young Canadians. Her leadership and contributions have been recognized with numerous awards and accolades.

Additionally, Justine is a devoted supporter of her alma mater, contributing to diversity and inclusion initiatives and serving on the university's board and advisory board for the Telfer Business School.

JANET DONOVAN

Janet Donovan, the President and CEO of Girl Scouts in the Heart of Pennsylvania, is a retired U.S. Navy Rear Admiral with a distinguished career spanning over three decades. Her executive experience is rich in strategy development, talent management, and collaboration, making her a formidable leader in her field. Janet's background includes extensive professional development and executive training in areas such as strategic planning, communication, innovation, coalition-building, finance, cybersecurity, risk management, and ethics.

Holding a law degree from Case Western Reserve University and a Bachelor of Arts in Spanish from The College of Wooster, her educational journey is as impressive as her professional one. Janet has witnessed the transformative power of Girl Scouts in shaping young women's lives. She is a firm believer in the unique opportunities Girl Scouting offers, preparing the next generation of confident and capable leaders.

Listen to the podcast episode!

REFLECTION QUESTIONS

1. Can you think of a time when your passion for your work actually got in your way of success?

2. Justine speaks about the importance of curiosity as a leader. How does curiosity show up in your leadership style? How could you embrace more curiosity on a daily basis?

3. In her story, Janet reiterates the importance that individuals have to uphold the systems around them. Do you feel this responsibility to act with moral integrity inside the systems you work in? Has your integrity ever been challenged? Would you be willing to share that story?

4. Is there an industry or a field of study that you completely align with? What is it? Have you ever considered applying to work in that field? What holds you back?

EMBRACING CHALLENGE

Participants repeatedly took on challenging leadership roles for which they were underprepared, sometimes in fields where they had no prior experience. Participants chose to move out of roles in which they were comfortable and successful, and into roles that were uncomfortable for them, and which required them to stretch and grow to maintain their success.

AMBITION
by Sherry Schaefer

AS A KID, I loved a challenge. If someone said I couldn't do it, it just made me want to do it even more. And it always seemed I did things the unconventional way, and maybe that was to make the challenge even sweeter. I would set goals and then work hard to meet the challenge and, I would say, most of the time it worked out in my favor.

I remember being about twelve, and the school was taking my grade to the mountains to hike to the top. I wanted to go in the worst way. But the problem was, I was no athlete. Despite my thinking, I could win races; it was just not my forte. But hiking to the top of the mountain and being a part of something that "cool," now that was something I wanted to do. So when the teacher said only the top fifty athletes could go, well the challenge was set. When the teacher set up training sessions, I was there early and I worked hard, but I always seemed to be in last place. I was not to be deterred. That teacher, one of my favorites, was always pushing me, telling me that I could do it. His words of encouragement were a big help and, finally, when the last time trial was over, I had done it. I came in at number fifty! I could go on the trip.

The funny thing is, my idea of being at the top seemed to be about being on the podium or the best athlete. But what I didn't realize then was that wasn't what I was good at—I had other skills that were exemplary. I was a champion of spirit. That school trip I didn't come back as the first one to the top, nope! I came back with the award for Most Congenial, the one who was encouraging others who struggled to get up the hardest legs of the hike. I was a cheerleader for the underdog.

Fast forward twenty years and here I was, trying once again to reach what seemed just out of my grasp. It wasn't always easy and definitely not straightforward. I think as young professionals we believe that there is a straight and narrow path to where we want to be, and although it may be challenging, we are up for the challenge. But often the world has different ideas for us and we end up taking some side trails and some major shifts in the path, and yet I believe we get to where we need and should be in the end. For me, this was the case, most definitely.

A few years into my healthcare career as a recreation therapist, I realized I wanted to be at the decision-making table. I wanted to be a leader for the teams that made things happen in the hospital I worked at. At first it was just a manager position I dreamed of, but it soon shifted to executive level. It was a long way to go, and my dream to run a hospital was not going to be easy, especially since I wasn't in the traditional field of nursing. I really believed I had what it took to lead the staff of a center and make a difference for seniors in care. After some deep thought, I decided to take a giant leap and ask for a meeting with the CEO and find out what I would need to do to be in an executive leadership position.

Surprisingly, I was granted that meeting, so I was pretty excited and—let's just say—full of ego.

The day I had my meeting, I dressed extra smartly and made sure I arrived early. I wanted to make my best first impression. I sat down across from her noticing her tailored business suits and sensible but stylish pumps, and I took a big breath. After a few moments of me explaining how I love the organization, and how I wanted to move up into leadership, I asked her what she thought I would need to do to achieve this. She paused and then said, "It is just not possible. You would have needed to take a nursing degree and since that's not the case, you can't do it." I have to say, I was taken aback. Way back! Here I was a young, keen, thirty-year-old with ambitions to be on the executive team, and she, in three sentences, crushed that thought. My mouth dropped and I just looked at her, unable to say anything. I really thought she was more progressive. I knew that other organizations had non-nurse managers and they were excelling. I thought we as an organization had moved past this old style of thinking, that only nurses were qualified to serve as leaders within the hospital.

I don't think I felt my full shock in her unexpected response until I had left the building. I was so disappointed. I had a university degree in an allied health discipline with half my courses in business and organizational management; I really felt I had leadership qualities that could grow with opportunities. I knew I would have hard work to get to the leadership role I wanted, and I really thought she would tell me what steps I would have to take and keep me in mind for special projects that would help me grow my skills. This answer she gave was a shut door. It was not the answer I thought I would get.

After a few days of licking my wounds, I realized I had a choice: leave the organization or dig in. So I dug in. Like many other times, the challenge was not easy, seemingly just out of reach but somehow, I would get there. I guess I could have decided to go back and become a nurse, but starting over wasn't my style. Instead, I would find another way. I really believed then and now that leadership is a skill unto itself and excelling as a nurse, in this case, was not a guarantee of being a great leader.

I searched for months for the best master's program, looking for something that was a good fit for me, something that I could take that would increase my knowledge and skills in leadership. I would show my commitment to the organization and my value as a leader. A year later, I was beginning my first master's in health service administration classes. Once again, I was on a path up the mountain!

In the meantime, other opportunities at work arose here and there, and I kept offering my assistance. This strategy had to pay off. I would not be deterred, and I was not afraid of hard work and extra hours to be part of special projects on top of my therapist role. Some days were hard, and I would wonder if it all would pay off, but I wanted to show them I had what it took. I would show the executive and CEO that I could, I would, and I did.

If a tree falls in the woods along your path, do we turn around and give up on the walk? No, we find another way. We create a new path to get us to the other side. Learning to get past the "no's" has been not once, twice, or even just three times in my career. And despite the numerous no's, I have stayed thirty-five-plus years in my organization. Don't get me wrong, I have had an amazing career, but it was due in large part to my persistence in a set goal and, like the teacher when I was twelve, the support of good and encouraging mentors. This has been what kept me going and made all the difference.

My vision of leadership at the executive table and desire to make a difference was my driver. It was what motivated me to push myself.

It has always been important to me to show people that I could; that it was more than just my education, more than just my degree. My totality of skills and strengths are based on education, experience, and my overall life philosophy. This is why I wanted and truly needed to move past the no's.

I volunteered for committees focused on organizational team building, I stayed late to help with special events, and I offered to help with big fundraising projects which often meant extra time working on them after the kids were in bed. Putting in the extras I was sure would pay off.

After doing two special assignments of major depth, and a new CEO coming on board with a different approach, I was finally given a chance. I was asked to manage a care unit in our long-term care hospital. I knew that there would have been some heavy closed-door conversation over this prior to the offer as I wasn't a nurse. There would be some who thought it wasn't a good idea, but I was so happy to have the opportunity. I had made a significant milestone! Once again, I would show them I could, and I would.

But the journey wasn't over. Apparently, I still had lessons to learn.

You have to remember, hospitals and senior care centers are rich with tradition. New thinking is not easy, and change is often challenged. Here's how it went:

Day 1: I proudly moved my things into my new manager's office, setting it up with care. I wanted to have that open door, welcoming atmosphere for my staff and patients. And, at the same time, make it obvious that I was serious about my role.

Day 2: I held my first team meeting where I told the team, "You can come to me with anything. I am here for you." They all smiled at me, but no comments or words were spoken. Little did I realize they were not happy that I was there. Why? You guessed it—I was not a nurse! Are you kidding? Not this again. Ten years since I had that dreadful conversation with the past CEO, and I was still facing the same old-fashioned thinking.

Day 3: The nurse from my team came to me to share "the team's thoughts." She simply said, "The nursing team won't be coming to you. You are not a nurse. So I'll just be in charge and let you know what we are doing." Flabbergasted, I tried to redirect this, but the words were not coming to me easily. I was frustrated to say the least.

I held it in until I got to the car that day and then the tears just flowed. I worked so hard to get here and for what? They don't respect me, and I wasn't sure they ever would.

Day 4: Self-talk. You can do this—just figure out how. Then I remembered a few years back my husband had been asked to take over a manager role in an area he was not familiar with. His background was in an allied area, but he did not have the specific background of this department. When he asked his boss why him, the director said, "I am not hiring you to *be a specialist* in the department. I am hiring you to *manage the specialists you have working for you.*" These words of wisdom became my guiding principle as a manager. And with the support of our hospital director and some excellent colleagues who stood by me, I made it through the next few months.

I was able to sit down with the team and set up some working relationships that acknowledged their strengths and skills and outlined mine. From that point on, we had one of the best teams in the center. Five more years snuck by and the joy and ease of having such a terrific team made for an amazing leadership experience. I truly felt I had arrived and my goal to eventually oversee a hospital was only one step away.

Then it came. The unexpected door that opened. The unmapped path to the top of the mountain.

It was November 2012 when I got a call from the organization's CEO asking me to call her back when I had a moment. I was two levels below her, so I was surprised to get this message directly and not through my director. I took a deep breath, unsure of what she wanted, or worse yet, what I had done, and I returned her call.

I listened to her carefully. "Would you consider a secondment? Would you move to the corporate office and take on a long-term fundraising project?" Really? Now? Was she serious? I had worked so hard to overcome obstacles and old-fashioned beliefs to get to where I was as a care manager. I really felt my destiny was to be a hospital administrator and this last role of care manager was leading me nicely into that place of executive leadership. Now she was asking me to change gears and take something on that I was familiar with from my major projects but was so very different from the path I had set for myself. I needed a moment—well, actually, I asked her for a few days to think on it.

With some good guidance and encouragement from my mentors and inner circle colleagues who knew me best, I considered the leap. It was an unexpected opportunity to leap-frog to the corporate office, and possibly put me at the executive table, just in a different capacity than I had been planning for. So I agreed to take it on, but I had a few caveats. Truly, if after a year I preferred being in my previous role, I wanted the option to return to it. I did not want to fully give up on the career trajectory I had originally set before myself. So with this CEO's promise that I could return if it wasn't all that she thought it would be, I moved my office to the downtown corporate location.

Once again, the arrival into a new role was not what I could have imagined. Again, I was faced with naysayers and doubters. I think this was about the time I first heard the term "impostor syndrome." Except for me, it wasn't that I didn't believe, well not initially; it was that people around me imposed that kind of thinking on me. It doesn't take long for that kind of pressure and those comments to start to impact what you think, causing you to believe you don't have what it takes. Am I an impostor in this role? These are the times we have to dig in and dig deep to find the courageous leadership we have within us. Easier said than done on some days, but some regrouping and good support from mentors and trusted colleagues can help. Here's what happened at my arrival to corporate office life.

Day 1: Eager to excel and committed to my organization, I walked into the corporate office with my business suit and lipstick and a box of family pictures for my desk. I had arrived! Again. The first person I met pointed me in the direction of my office. It was the farthest corner of the floor with no one around me. Basically, it was the closest location to the storage room and the fire escape. I was disheartened but it was only day one I told myself. Things would improve . . . or so I hoped.

Day 2: I walked through the office introducing myself, eager to meet new team members, several of which barely lifted their heads to acknowledge me. Hmmm . . . is this a place I want to be in? I thrive on teamwork and positive energy, and this just didn't seem to be it. I carried on.

Day 3: A coffee room conversation about who I was, and why was I "given" the role. I realized from the questions that I was being asked that people at the corporate office did not agree with me being in this role. The naysayers were speaking loud and clear. And some of them were just plain unkind about it.

Days 4–10: More of the same. Here is where my discouragement and self-doubt kicked in. My resiliency to the obvious unkindness and office bullying was faltering. Did I make the right decision to move to this role? I think many people have these moments, and it so often feels so personal. I am by nature a people person, and this state of isolation that I was being handed was causing me to want to tuck tail and retreat. But here's where the words of my kind and wise grade school teacher came to me: "You can make it if you work hard." And the words from a lovely grandmother, long gone by then, who always said, "You need to kill them with kindness." So for the next three months that's exactly what I did. I worked hard every day, with large goals in my front view, and the challenge of turning around these overly unkind naysayers. They would not break me. Some days were torture, but I persevered.

This next moment was exactly what I needed to get through this crazy situation. I was on my last day before a winter getaway, and my CEO, who had convinced me to take on this role, came by to see me. I knew she supported me, but I wasn't sure she was aware of all the office antics that were causing me angst. She simply asked me how it was going. I couldn't help it; the tears just came. I really tried to be professional and not show my inner thoughts and there I was doing exactly what I said I wouldn't do. With such kindness, she took a pause and then gave me some incredibly reassuring words. I was so grateful. I took a deep breath and did what I always did—decided to come back with some reframing of my approach to the situation and not let it deter me.

I returned from the much-needed vacation and knew then that if I just stayed focused on my role and the work I needed to do, these sideline issues would not interfere; at least I refused to let them. I believed in the CEO and her vision, so I needed to make it work. I am happy to say the big corporate project was a huge success and we raised millions to rebuild dining rooms in our older hospitals. I did stay at the corporate office permanently, and finally landed that position at the decision-making table as an executive leader.

Thinking back on these specific moments, I do wonder how thirty-five years has gone by, all in one organization. The culture of the organization overall was terrific and the cause we served meant a great deal to me. My passion for our work was deep.

When I say I grew up in the organization, I am not referring to my youthful start there, but instead I am thinking about the growth and wisdom I gained through my experiences. My leadership journey has evolved because of these experiences, and I believe every future leader needs to go through good and challenging times, if only to learn. Understanding what shakes our core beliefs strengthens our commitment to those beliefs. Gaining skills from experiences, not just books and theory, is how we add to our leadership toolbox.

I see the next generation of leaders and now stop to acknowledge their good work, their moments of excellence, and their moments of growth and reflection. It is my and my generation of leaders' responsibility to mentor and share wisdom so they can grow into their leadership. I want my story to be heard so that young leaders, and even seasoned leaders, know that these challenges, although they cause discomfort as they unfold, are necessary to strengthen the individual. They must be viewed as opportunities to improve.

Being told no doesn't mean stop and retreat. There are always mountains to climb, treks to reach a destination, and trees that fall on the paths. It's how we view the challenges, the journeys, and what seems like the impassable. The elderly people I worked with in the hospital know that this means stop, reconfigure, be creative, and move forward. That's how our communities through the generations were built and that's how we as leaders need to view our work. Maintaining a positive work culture, knowing who your supporters are, and gaining support from those you know believe in you. These things will all add up to success and best strategies to maneuver around the obstacles that impact the journey.

When I think about the career mountain I had climbed, and how others face similar challenges and obstacles, I think about the wisdom from my elders who gave me my passion to serve in the healthcare industry: "Where there's a will there most definitely is a way!"

IDENTITY
by Heather Bach

SIMPLY PUT, I am more of the little engine that could than I am a leader. Always doing something for someone but not the decision-maker. I would describe myself as nobody special doing a great job and making an impact on my community almost daily. Always up for a challenge, pushing forward, trying to improve, and striving to be worthy of the leader title.

To me a leader is someone that is well respected with a high level of integrity. Someone who empowers the people around them and celebrates everyone's success. Visually, I always picture a beautiful, high-class person with impeccable manners.

I never had a role model for leadership within any of my inner working circles throughout the course of my career; I just learned what kind of leader I didn't want to be through lived experience. My only hope was looking up to public figures as leaders, but that could be risky too. I was often disappointed by their lack of integrity. Basically, I learned to work hard, keep my head down, control all aspects of my business, and not count on anyone but myself. We used to call it "CYA"—cover your a$$.

I grew up in retail management. In my case, it was an eat-or-be-eaten kind of environment. You were on call 24/7, 365 days a year if you expected to have a secure position. You did what you were told and you did it now. It wasn't about growing the team but about growing the revenue and the profit. In short, it was leadership by intimidation.

I started working there as a young adult in an entry-level position within a department. After four months, I was promoted to assistant department manager. I did that for about two years before it was time for more; I needed a bigger challenge, and I wanted a department of my own.

I thought I was a great manager; I controlled productivity, I turned over great profits, but I didn't like the fact that good people were leaving and bad people kept getting the promotions. Staff were not being empowered to be their best selves, their ideas were ignored, and their loyalty to the organization taken advantage of instead of celebrated. That wasn't my idea of a great team.

I wanted to laugh and have fun with my colleagues. I wanted to work hard and support them whenever it was needed. Celebrate their success and try again with the failures. I wanted everyone to just be themselves.

In 2006 I was turned down from a leadership role. When I challenged the decision, I was told that I was the best candidate, but it would put too much stress on my family. Keeping in mind I had worked for this organization for fourteen years and never called in sick or been seriously disciplined. I knew what I was getting into. This was the beginning of the end for me at this organization.

Finally, I convinced leadership to promote me. I got the worst department in the organization, a department that wasn't making a profit, and I was told it would never make a profit—but here you go if you think you are so smart. You see, as a department manager, you received a 2 percent bonus from the profits your department made quarterly. Upper leadership also received a share of the profit you made. The pressure was on.

It took me two years to create a profit, and after four years I was bored again. Looking for a bigger challenge and more responsibility. As they say, be careful what you wish for. This time I got the challenge of a lifetime. Probably the one that shaped my leadership style the most. It wasn't big from a blueprint perspective but it had many moving parts and 300 percent more staff. The revenue was stable and the potential to make a profit was grand. The scary part was that this department had a history of turning over its managers, and not many people survived. One of the organization's philosophies was "up, up, and out." Meaning we will promote you until you are in over your head. Staff turned over like a pair of socks.

There was no support. You had to figure it out on your own.

The job paid well and they reminded us regularly that we were no one special and that no one in the outside world would hire us. Our skills were not transferable and even if we could find another job, we would never earn that wage on the outside. That's why it took me so long to get the courage to try something new. I was a fighter, stubborn and relentless, but I wasn't growing—only the profits were growing.

I had a young family. I used to go to work at 8:00 a.m., work until 6:00 p.m., pick up kids, feed kids, get them to bed by 8:00 p.m. so I could go back to work until 10:00 or 11:00 p.m. Or else I brought the work home and did it in front of the TV while everyone slept. I really learned to count on myself and only myself. Stress levels were high all the time. I'm not sure how I managed but after seven years it was time for a change.

Looking at myself in the mirror one day I realized I didn't like the person looking back at me. I had become a coldhearted, emotionless robot. Not the person or the leader that I wanted for myself or my daughters.

My family was, is, and always has been important to me, but my career had pulled me away. It was time for me to put my family first. I also wanted to be treated better, and to be respected for my work, dedication, and loyalty.

I wanted to be a leader. One who allowed people to be themselves, make mistakes, and grow. If they, too, wanted to put their families first, I wanted to be the kind of leader that let them do that. And I couldn't do any of those things here.

I hadn't applied for a job in nearly fifteen years or even really ever had an interview. I didn't even know where to start. At that time, jobs were still posted in our local newspaper. It got to the point where I was applying for almost anything. At least the interview would give me experience if nothing else.

Finally, I found a posting for a local charity looking for a fundraiser. To my surprise, I was even granted an interview. Funny story: I still have the suit jacket that I wore to that interview. I consider it a good luck charm that I might need again someday. Hopefully, it doesn't go out of style.

I grew up in a family that always volunteered. My grandmother worked with the Canadian Cancer Society, and my grandfather was involved in minor sports and started our community's first-ever food bank. My parents were involved in local service groups. Giving back, organizing events, fundraising, and volunteering were part of my everyday life. I just thought that is what you did. I had no idea you could get paid to be a fundraiser—what a great surprise.

I am not sure I really thought out my plan, but I knew this was an opportunity to grow, learn, and make an impact on my community. It was about helping other people, which I loved to do. I started in the development department, but I made it clear I was not going to stay in that position forever—I wanted more. When I was asked the question, "Where do you see yourself in five years?" I told the executive director at the time that I would be sitting in their seat. That boldness was out of character for me, and I knew I had a lot to learn first.

It was a little over five years, but finally I had the opportunity to apply for the executive director role. I was confident in my knowledge and ability. I thought I would finally have the opportunity to build my own team, grow the organization, and make a real difference in my community. I would have the autonomy to make some large-scale decisions. I'd been bitten in the past by politics, so I knew I needed to be careful.

When I was offered the position of executive director, I thought finally someone believes in me. Someone other than me knows I am capable of this amazing position; I am going to do great things. After the offer, the next words spoken to me were, "And if you screw this up, you will never work in this town again."

The wind in my sail had just been released. What did I just get myself into? Was I back in a toxic work environment? Was there going to be no autonomy and would this be more leadership by intimidation?

That single sentence made me revert to the manager I used to be in my old position. I had to prove myself—back to my comfort zone, head down—and work hard, grind, and trust no one. My reputation was on the line, so how could I trust anyone else? As an organization, we weren't growing; we were stable, we were getting done what needed to get done, but nothing more. I felt like I was on a hamster wheel, too caught up doing the basics to innovate, fix anything, or try anything new. I was just copying someone else's playbook.It wasn't until I hit rock bottom (as I like to call it) that the tides started to change. Just before COVID-19 in March 2020, I lost my whole team over the course of a couple of months for various and different reasons. I found myself alone—I was literally the only employee. Well, if there is one thing that I am good at it is remaining calm in a crisis. I called a temp agency and begged them to send me anybody that could answer the phone for me so I could move forward on the other tasks.

I had events to organize and host, mailouts to complete, daily operations—oh, and hire new staff. There was no time to think, to worry, or to even second guess myself because I had to get to work. Being in this position forced me to fix the things that were broken, develop new systems, and take ownership. I didn't have time to run through how it had been done before. I had to trust myself, my instincts, and own my knowledge.

This was either going to work, or I was going to fail badly. And I was determined not to fail. It was time to build back a team, and this time I was going to do it my way. Slowly, the pieces started to fall into place and the results started to come in.

I got brave and took a chance on hiring the right people, people that had more or different skills than myself. I up-leveled my team and together we built a strong core team that continues to grow and learn day after day.

The first year that we started breaking records was so exciting it felt surreal. I was almost in tears as we celebrated at a team lunch. Did we just get lucky? Was this a one-off? The beautiful part is that it was just the start. We continue to break revenue records; we continue to grow and level up as a team and an organization.

When you surround yourself with the right people, empower them, help them grow in the direction that is best for them and their well-being, the money comes without even having to try. It is no longer work but fun activities engaging with people that are making a difference in lives in our community every day. Isn't that what leadership is all about?

Life is full of experiences that help us grow if we choose to learn the lessons. Now I actually enjoy making mistakes because it gives way for more growth. Grit has served me well, and time has helped me step back and gain perspective through self-reflection.

As I write this, I realize I am a leader. Writing this chapter has allowed me to slow down and see myself in a new way. Now that I have become a mentor, it is time for me to step into my leadership identity and truly see myself in this new light: no longer the little engine that could, but a confident and capable leader.

～ MEET THE AUTHORS ～

SHERRY SCHAEFER, MHS

Sherry Schaefer has dedicated her career to geriatric care, specializing in senior health and wellness, event planning, and fund development. Over the past decade, she has become a pivotal figure in mentoring professionals within the healthcare and fund development sectors. Her pursuit of a master's in health administration, with a focus on leadership and team-building strategies, has deepened her expertise in mentorship and team development.

Sherry's advancement in the healthcare sector can be attributed to her expertise in negotiation, leveraging, and focused networking. These skills have been instrumental in leading highly productive and effective teams and achieving remarkable organizational outcomes. Her leadership style is characterized by her remarkable ability to motivate her teams toward shared goals.

An established speaker, presenter, and host, Sherry excels in engaging audiences at educational institutes, major fundraisers, virtual sessions, and national conferences. Her ability to integrate powerful storytelling into her presentations enables her to connect deeply with audiences, inspiring change and action.

Sherry is a co-coach at Chavender, where she continues to share her insights and experience in mentorship.

HEATHER BACH

Heather Bach stands out as a dedicated and passionate executive in healthcare philanthropy. Known for her fierce independence and unwavering commitment to excellence, Heather approaches every challenge with creativity and determination, consistently finding innovative ways to achieve her goals and boost revenue.

Her loyalty extends deeply to her community, family, and anyone eager to delve into the world of philanthropy. Heather's dedication to giving back is exemplified through her active involvement in volunteerism. She holds significant roles as a board member of several esteemed organizations, including AFP (Association of Fundraising Professionals), AHP (Association for Healthcare Philanthropy), CGAP (Certified Government Auditing Professional), and her local Rotary club.

Listen to the podcast episode!

REFLECTION QUESTIONS

1. Can you think of a time when you took on a role that you were underprepared for? Or maybe you had no experience in that field? How did you manage those first few months when you were feeling uncomfortable?

2. Sherry uses the term "champion of spirit" to describe what she was good at. Who in your life champions the underdog, cheering everyone on from the sidelines?

3. Have you ever been told a flat-out no to a request you made? What did you do next? Can you share that story?

4. Workplaces have many different cultures. Have you ever worked in a place where people were unkind to each other at work? How did that affect you? Did you try and overcome it? Or did you leave that organization? What would you do if you were leading that organization?

5. Do you think of yourself as a persistent person? Can you think of something specific that you did not give up on, even though the probability of success was low? Have you ever thought of that as a skill?

6. One of the core elements of Heather's story is the amount of grit and determination she shows. Do you have grit and determination? How does it show up for you at work?

GLASS CLIFF ASSIGNMENTS

Women are more likely to be named CEO for an organization in a precarious financial situation. This phenomenon is conceptualized as a glass cliff and is particularly true in nonprofits. Almost all those facing glass cliff situations were able to successfully navigate the path to bring their organizations to more structurally, financially, and culturally sound places.

FAILING FORWARD
by Mojdeh Cox

The Walkout

I STILL REMEMBER the contrast of the cold, sterile air inside the building and the near-suffocating heat of that summer day. The day that everything turned upside down. Nothing made sense, including the calm that overtook me as I stared at the curb waiting for my spouse, Dave, to pick me up. I don't remember what I told him on the phone when I asked him to come back to the office only hours after he had dropped me off. I remember seeing the expression on his face as he approached. No words were exchanged between us because, after twenty-three years, he knew I was heartbroken and confused just by looking at me.

Minutes earlier, I had been escorted by six members of the board of directors out of the meeting to my office, where they watched me gather my personal items, then through the lobby, out the front doors, and across the sidewalk to the very edge of the organization's property line. The board members surrounded me in horseshoe formation while I awkwardly fumbled with my purse and tote bag. And just like that, at the peak of my career and only fourteen months into my tenure as CEO, I was exited from my role. Without notice. Without process. Without cause.

It was one of those moments that will forever define my life. I use words like "before" and "after" the walkout when I talk about my career. It changed my life personally and professionally and was a classic example of the glass cliff experience: where women are more often appointed or promoted to precarious leadership roles during times of crisis or high risk. The glass cliff presents differently when examined through the eyes of a woman of color. For women of color, the glass cliff is further compounded by the intersecting biases of gender and race. This makes the obstacles we encounter even more challenging. Women who step into glass cliff experiences have a predetermined high probability of failure. Placing women of color in leadership positions where failure is more likely perpetuates the negative stereotypes and biases that women of color are actively counteracting by stepping into these leadership roles in the first place! They take the job because it is an opportunity to change the stereotypes, but quickly realize they have (often) been set up to fail before they even start.

Let me back up to the beginning of this story. At the height of the pandemic, I began my journey as a nonprofit CEO. Within ten days of my arrival, we held our annual general meeting. There were a lot of changes at the board level: six new board members were appointed, and a new chair and vice chair were elected. The massive changes at the leadership level created a level of instability that I had questions about. I had reservations, sensing that there were some fundamental challenges, but I was also determined to make this opportunity work. After all, I had moved my family over 550 kilometers for this job. I was ready to put in the time and effort to make this work.

Over the course of the next fourteen months, I navigated the inevitable elements of this glass cliff experience. I was conscious of how close to the edge I was all the time. I was convinced that I could change my own reality and placed unrealistic expectations on myself. Even though I could see that I was standing at the edge of a cliff, I did my best to somehow chart a solid path forward without infrastructure, without mechanisms in place to support my leadership.

Despite all of these barriers, we were successful in rebuilding the organizational culture; we deployed a shared leadership model among all our senior women leadership team; and after years of internal and community-level advocacy, we rolled out and implemented decent work measures. This included developing pay principles including establishing pay transparency, a practice of openly sharing information about employees' salaries, wages, and benefits within an organization, allowing employees to understand the compensation structure, thereby fostering a more equitable and fair work environment. I was exhausted *and* I recognized that these milestones warranted celebration. I was complicit in my own exhaustion. I had placed the burden of "fixing" things on myself, the very person that the organization had set up to fail.

I had made a conscious choice to shift my career from labor relations to the nonprofit sector. At the time, the Canadian Labour Congress, my former employer, was reverting back to an outdated business unionism structure that eliminated their anti-racism and human rights, health and safety, and environment and international departments. I wanted a deeper connection to the people impacted by my work and chose to take the leap and transition into the community nonprofit sector.

The selection process for my role as CEO had been rigorous: many touch points with the selection committee and executive search firm and phone calls to *ten* of my references. From start to finish, it took the committee nearly five months to finally offer me the job. With this offer in hand, I brought my family together to wrap our minds and hearts around the opportunity. The timing was not ideal—it was at the height of the pandemic. As a family, we reviewed the pros and cons of the situation, and what we would need to let go of to make this opportunity work. My twins were only six years old at the time, my middle child was ten years old, and my oldest son was nineteen, wrapping up his first year of university. When it came time to vote, we were all in. We were ready for the move from Ottawa to Southwestern Ontario, knowing that COVID-19 restrictions would make this move memorable, to say the least. We were moving back to a town that was familiar to us— my husband and I had lived and worked there for eighteen years before our time in Ottawa.

I thought back to that family vote as I stood on the curb, unusually calm considering the situation. My family had invested in *me* and took a chance because they believed in me. The weight of disappointing them was crushing.

My identity was so intricately woven into my leadership and community roles. I would feel bewildered and burdened for weeks to come. I had no energy or imagination for what could possibly be on the other side of this hurdle.

The Depression Hammock

For the next two months I would turn to Dave at least three times a week and ask, "Did that really happen? Did I get walked off my job?" He is no stranger to the way I process things. After walking with me for over two decades through hardships, Dave is familiar with how I process, carry, and work through my life lessons. The walkout was so shocking that we both thought that there would come a moment when I would move past the phase of heaviness and confusion and *really* react. Maybe I would get angry, maybe I would cry. Anything other than this blanket of heaviness wrapping around me. We were both holding our breath, waiting for the moment when I could finally say I had "hit rock bottom." I could sense that all Dave wanted to do was to wrap me up in Bubble Wrap and protect me. From the world and from myself.

Bubble Wrap protects. What Dave chose to do instead helped me process my experiences. One day he came home with a gift, and he led me into our backyard. There are two beautiful and massive pine trees that stand at the back of our large property. In between these majestic trees, Dave had hung a single hammock chair.

"I got you this chair. Let's call it your depression hammock. It's a place you can go when you need time alone. You can look toward the house or flip it and look out into the woods. Let this be your space to just be," he said.

These were loving words, especially for a true introvert like me. I cherish alone time because it's how I recharge. The walkout happened early in the summer, and since school was out, I found myself with four sets of young eyes on me. Subconsciously, I was holding off processing what had happened. If I was unable to take the time to process this experience, I would be unable to pick myself up and start thinking about my future.

I spent countless hours on the depression hammock. I used it as a place to retreat and shut out the noise. As time went on, the depression hammock became my place for reflection.

It was late fall, and although the trees in the woods still held their vibrant colors, I knew this would be one of my last reflection sessions on the hammock for the season. That day, I asked myself a long overdue question: What do you need right now to regain balance?

The realization finally came. I couldn't strive to regain balance because I had never actually had balance. This was a hard truth for me to accept. I had completely intertwined who I was and what I did for a living together. I had to find a new way to approach the work that I loved, and I needed to accept that I had lost my sense of self and my zest for life in the weeks following the walkout.

The Balancing Act

This realization prompted a poignant memory for me. Two weeks prior to the walkout, my daughter approached me as I was entering the house and she jumped on me, gave me a big hug, and said, "Thank you for coming home early!" It was after 7:00 p.m., and I remembered that I had left the house at 6:00 a.m. that morning. I was instantly ashamed. My daughter thought that 7:00 p.m. was *early*? I knew that this was not the way I wanted to model the role of work for my kids.

I justified my terrible habits of overextending myself as though I was an exception to the rule. I told myself that this was the price I paid for working in the community and impact sector. I perpetuated a false and dangerous narrative to justify the absent boundaries between myself, my work, and my community roles.

I didn't yet believe that doing the inner work that would allow me to give myself permission to rest and create healthy boundaries would help me have more impact. This is especially important when holding a position of power and authority; everyone looks up to their leader to see what they are doing, and what's acceptable at the organizational level.

Giving myself grace was part of the process of learning about balance. It was hard to find empathy for myself because I didn't recognize myself after the walkout. How could I? I was wedged between the shock of being terminated unexpectedly in such a humiliating way, the shame that comes with being disposed of as a racialized woman CEO, and the guilt of letting my family down as I witnessed them adjust to the financial implications of my job loss. Not only did I not recognize myself, but I was also terrified of reverting to the old version of me, the one that pushed herself so hard, the one that had no empathy for herself.

I accepted the fact that I was grieving. I was not only grieving the job I loved, the colleagues I respected, and the community I built around my profession, I was also grieving a version of me that no longer existed.

Glass cliff scenarios for women of color generally include lateral violence and internalized hate. Lateral violence emerges when individuals within an oppressed group perpetuate oppression by inflicting abusive behavior on each other. This misguided expression of frustration is aimed at fellow peers or community members rather than addressing the primary oppressors. Internalized hate occurs when an individual develops ideas, beliefs, actions, and behaviors that support or collude with racism. Both are a byproduct of colonialism. These concepts were not new to me. I spent the greater part of my career before this role researching and developing anti-racism and anti-oppression training, frameworks, and content.

In some ways, it was easier to hold space and forgive the board members who conducted the walkout than it was to forgive myself. I empathized with the notion that internalized racism was being projected onto the organization and that this was a subconscious action. I knew I needed to forgive myself. But how? I kept asking myself, "Why did you ignore the red flags?" I blamed myself for the walkout and for making my family suffer the consequences.

My ego was trying to protect me. It was trying to fool my mind into thinking that I had control over the actions of others. My ego stopped me from moving past blame, even when I was blaming myself for failing to act on the red flags that I saw but ignored. I needed to find a way to forgive myself so I could begin to heal.

My healing began once I acknowledged the connection between grief and forgiveness. It took time for me to forgive myself for my role in the experience, but I did it. I knew I would need great courage to strike the balance I wanted, needed, and deserved going forward.

Redefining Success in Leadership

I knew I would need courage to pursue the balance I yearned for. It would require me to challenge deeply ingrained societal beliefs and expectations that had held me captive for far too long. Traditional leadership paradigms reference failure as something to be avoided rather than be embraced or expected. Similarly, success is framed around "being perfect." The reality is that the journey between victories is anything but linear; there are successes and failures, and the steps are rarely linear. The leadership journey has its own organic sequence.

I now believe that failing is an important step toward great leadership. Failing forces leaders to be humble. Humility enables leaders to make more informed decisions, inspire others, and drive meaningful and sustainable change. Failure also helps leaders evolve and learn critical lessons like how to listen to others. The old leadership paradigms aligned failure with demonstrating weakness. Embracing failure as a natural part of the leadership journey requires emotional maturity and courage. This is called failing forward. I was intentionally reframing failure as a valuable and necessary part of my journey and growth. I decided I would emerge on the other side of this experience with a bolder version of myself.

I knew I had two immediate goals: secure meaningful employment and do it in a way where I did not slide backward into the version of myself that had stood at that curb. I thought I would end up with a similar role in the sector and had started the executive search process when I received a phone call from a nonprofit board chair I had collaborated with in my previous role. This chair invited me to continue my work with their organization as a strategic adviser on subjects that I cared about: pay transparency, shared leadership, and more. The invitation gave birth to Cox & Co., a family-run, values-driven, boutique consulting firm specializing in ethical governance, strategic planning, coaching and advising, labor relations, and policy and advocacy work.

For a decade and a half, I had been consulting off the side of my desk but had not relied on it as my core income and full-time business. I realize it seems counterintuitive to invite more uncertainty into my life by becoming an entrepreneur, but after deep thought and planning, I was actually really excited about the possibility. I applied all my energy to make it a reality. And I did.

My eldest son and I now operate Cox & Co. I am so grateful for the phone call that changed the way I looked at the future. That invitation led to several more calls. Many of the conversations began with, "I was following your work. Can you help us in the same way?" Within a few months of opening our doors, we were booked with clients until the end of the year.

Full Circle

Failing forward into entrepreneurship has undeniably given me the greatest gifts, and for multiple compelling reasons. Running my own business has granted me a newfound sense of tranquility and inherent security, especially when it comes to addressing workplace violence and the traumatic experiences associated with glass cliff assignments. Not only does it allow me to persistently pursue my passion for collaborating with organizations and their leaders to maximize their impact through an equity lens, but it also enables me to maintain a healthy balance by establishing clear boundaries between my personal identity and professional work.

Failing into entrepreneurship as an accidental founder has afforded me the opportunity to have a positive impact on my community and provide for my family without compromising my values. I am now anticipating the challenges ahead on my journey in entrepreneurship, and I recognize that embracing both the failures and the reflection that must follow is what shapes hearts, minds, and perspectives.

As I sit on the hammock—it has become my sacred space for envisioning, seeking peace, and finding contentment—I reflect on the remarkable journey that has brought me from that curb on a scorching day to where I am today. I have emerged as a seasoned leader and entrepreneur, overcoming pain and humiliation by reshaping my perspective on failure, and hence, reshaping my life.

THE GALLERY
by Olinda Casimiro

IN JUNE 2017, I landed a role as executive director of a small, rural, public art gallery—the Art Gallery of Northumberland (AGN) in Cobourg, Ontario. I had spent the previous twenty-two years moving through various roles at a larger regional gallery forty minutes down the highway in the small city of Oshawa, an experience I hoped would serve me well in Northumberland County. But the gallery I had left had a robust staff of museum and arts professionals, strong relationships with donors and government funding bodies, and a clear sense of its purpose within its community. As I would realize within weeks of accepting the job as AGN's new executive director (ED), it had been years since my new professional home had had any of these things.

The purpose of a public art gallery is to educate the public and to collect and promote art. Commercial galleries act like agents, connecting artists to the collectors who buy their work. But public galleries have a broader role: they help define what art is for and within their communities, and they can support artists in creating work that may not be a good fit for a commercial space. Founded in 1960 as the Cobourg Art Gallery, the AGN had spent most of its history doing exactly that. It had always been a collecting institution, and by the time it moved in 1977 to its current location inside Cobourg's magnificent nineteenth-century town hall, it was thriving. It had 2,300 square feet of exhibition space, a climate-controlled art storage vault, and a regular exhibition program that reflected the region as well as its collection and services. As it rounded the corner into its sixth decade, nothing in its history would have suggested it was heading for a crisis that would leave it struggling to survive.

The origins of this crisis were mundane—the kinds of misunderstandings and differences in expectations that often create friction between a nonprofit's board and those managing day-to-day operations. Normally, clear communication and the occasional personnel change is enough to resolve these conflicts, but in the AGN's case, neither proved possible. The former director struggled to convey the gallery's needs to a board that, while well-intentioned, lacked experience in arts administration and the management of an art collection. As things became untenable, and the pressure on them mounted, the director's focus shifted from institutional stewardship to self-preservation. Any communication that had previously existed broke down. By the time I was brought in, the previous director and the board were long gone, and with them sailed the bulk of the AGN's institutional knowledge.

During the interview process, it became clear the AGN was in trouble and although the opportunity seemed daunting, I was excited for the challenge of turning it around. What I discovered in my first few days on the job was that the situation was much, much worse than I'd imagined.

Not only had its staff been decimated, the gallery's practical situation was dire. The organization was in substantial debt, and it was no longer operating as a public art gallery. Twelve important works of art had been deaccessioned from a collection that was in total disarray. The director's office was packed with stacks of exhibition proposals and the unfinished paperwork of a string of temporary EDs.

A working board of directors and small team of volunteers had mostly managed to keep things running, but their experience was in business, not running public institutions. When funds dried up, they drew on what they knew to fill the gaps. The gallery had a main street gift shop in a neighboring town and had begun selling artwork, but it no longer paid artists to exhibit; and public programming—the school visits, summer camps, artist talks, and evening classes that once connected the AGN to its community—were a distant memory. The gallery had lost the public trust and regaining it would be daunting.

The seeming impossibility of the AGN's situation resonated with me. My grade twelve yearbook statement quoted Walter Bagehot, declaring that my "greatest pleasure in life [was] doing what people say you cannot do." In many ways, it felt like my entire career had been leading to this particular challenge. I had never intended to be an arts administrator. But as an eager university graduate, I took a short-term contract at the Robert McLaughlin Gallery (RMG) in Oshawa, Ontario. It was supposed to be a few months in a new (to me) world while I figured out what I actually wanted to do. But two days in, when the gallery's fifty-year-old director walked in wearing the latest fashion trend—a new pair of leather pants—a world of possibilities suddenly appeared. Here was a way to be a woman, a leader, a practical rock star. This was the kind of career I wanted.

As I worked my way up at the RMG, I got a comprehensive education in the running of a public gallery. A later director, successor to my original rock star role model, dedicated an afternoon a month to teaching me about the gallery's collection. Descending into the RMG vault, we'd debate the merits of various pieces. He shared his compassion, empathy, and thoughtfulness toward art and artists, and I began to see patterns and connections: donors' tastes, links between teachers and students, artists who were married to each other—it was fascinating.

I had grown up going to galleries and museums; I knew what I liked, and I had some general art historical knowledge. But as the months wore on, I started to understand the differences between individual taste and institutional responsibility. The collection wasn't about what my boss or any of his predecessors liked the most—though he and I had favorite pieces. It existed to help the community understand its past, connect to its present, and imagine its future. The collection needed to be able to tell stories about and through art that resonated with the people who came through the RMG's doors every day. The director needed to understand this mission, but so did every other staff member. And, as I experienced those afternoons in the vault, one of the best ways to build that understanding was through generosity of donors. Meanwhile, the many women who made up the rest of the staff taught me what it meant to balance a career with family and a personal life—not a new concept, of course, but it was new to me. There was a professional kindness and respect that ran through the organization, qualities that I honed to develop my own leadership style: I lead with collaboration and empathy.

Sifting through the papers documenting the AGN's previous five years, it was hard not to compare it to the RMG. Luckily, I met early on with the head of communications at a larger not-for-profit who offered me some sage advice: "You are going to want to change everything. Introduce change slowly or they will politely invite you to leave." The AGN was struggling, but that it had survived at all was thanks to the volunteers who had believed it was worth saving. Big changes were necessary, but I needed to convince those who had seen the gallery through its worst to move through change with me. If I couldn't, in a few months all of us—me, them, the gallery we cared about—could be gone.

After gleaning what I could from the documents that charted the course of the crisis, I boxed them up and sent them to storage. Then I began, slowly, to change everything. First, I reorganized the office. Out into the main gallery went the piles of forgotten proposals, five filing cabinets full of out-of-date paperwork, and everything else I could move. What could be sent to storage went to storage, what could be tossed got tossed. Once I had some breathing space, I addressed the gallery itself. The walls were a pale dirty yellow with hunter green trim, so I found four volunteers to paint them white—a blank canvas to begin a new chapter.

I was feeling rather accomplished after those first few weeks, but as I began to fully understand the AGN's financial risk and vulnerability, I knew the next step would be much harder. A focused examination of the finances revealed that the gallery had zero money. And a gallery with zero money cannot afford a paid staff. Two months after I started, I was forced to say an emotional goodbye to my one and only employee, a talented, energetic young woman who, as an artist herself, was passionate about the gallery. It was, and remains, one of the hardest things I have ever had to do.

With the gallery pared back as much as possible, I was finally ready to start the process of rebuilding. Slow change, but quickly—or, as I started to say, slow at the speed of lightning! First, I needed to address the budget. The AGN had funding suspended from major stakeholders, and one important suspension with implications for its ability to get that funding back. Its Category A designation, which indicated that it was able to ensure the long-term preservation of cultural property, i.e., the most important works in its collection, had been suspended. It took six months of perseverance, diligence, and ensuring compliance to reinstate it, but once I had, accessing funding would be the next step and the AGN became a lot less risky. Leveraging the gallery's reclaimed cultural importance secured a major funder, which then helped support grant applications at the provincial and federal levels.

Government support meant the AGN once again had a semblance of financial stability. But to survive in the long term, it also needed a real investment from a wider pool of stakeholders. It became clear to me very early on that the AGN's collection was primarily donations by the community. I was struck by how those gifts linked the gallery to the history of Northumberland County. Cobourg was a significant town in the 1800s, and many wealthy Americans had built grand summer homes nearby. In the vault, I discovered nineteenth-century portraits of important local figures and even a small drawing by the famous American painter John Singer Sargent. But the AGN's collection also reflected the community's more recent identity, including works by artists based in Cobourg and nearby Port Hope and eclectic personal collections.

For the gallery to thrive again, it would need to reestablish the kinds of connections that had built its collection. Personalized letters to our members and supporters, while time-consuming, seemed to be the right approach for this community. My focus was mending bridges with donors whose trust had been broken and establishing relations with senior leaders at the municipal level to demonstrate our viability. I also became a frequent visitor at the local cafés—amazing what a coffee chat offers! I wanted to understand people, the community, and how they thought—understand the role the gallery played in their lives or had played. What I really wanted was to dismantle long-held assumptions about what the AGN was and help others think about things in a different way.

The biggest issue at the AGN was a lack of institutional knowledge; not knowing how to function, it had lost all sense of mission. Removing the Do Not Touch and Quiet Please signs from the gallery walls made the space more inviting, but it needed much more. As I stepped up my efforts to build trust externally, I also needed to build trust internally, mentoring and coaching staff and volunteers—including the board of directors. Meeting regularly and individually with the remaining members of my team, I saw how deeply the crisis had affected them. The fifteen or so active volunteers were grateful to have me there, but they were uncertain of the change I was introducing. They had come so close to losing the gallery, it was difficult to let go of anything connected to that time of survival—even if it was holding the AGN back. The board, meanwhile, had taken on operational responsibilities well beyond their capabilities. I needed them to be vulnerable, acknowledge what wasn't working, and let me do my job. But they, like the volunteers, were stuck in something like a siege mentality—I needed to win them over.

When I arrived at the AGN, my task as ED had been to assess the damage head on and force everyone to acknowledge the reality of the situation, but now it shifted. It became about motivation, about empowering staff, volunteers, and engaging the community. Meetings always included a bit of social time, and that gave us the chance to learn about each other and build trust. By the fall, as I used a microphone to sing happy birthday to a volunteer who had just turned eighty, we reached a turning point. Laughing with them at my off-key rendition, I knew the volunteers were there to support and help me move the gallery forward. I never sang on the mic again, but the following spring, we invited a volunteer coordinator to strengthen our volunteer programs and begin volunteer recruitment.

New paint, new funding, a new crop of motivated and empowered volunteers—all of these were important. But an art gallery is not an art gallery if it doesn't show art. As I worked through the AGN's operational challenges, I was also sifting through the pile of unopened exhibition proposals that I had discovered in my office that first day on the job.

Most regional galleries offer a mix of curated shows: those that draw on works from a permanent collection, if the gallery has one; those presenting work by a single artist or group of artists curated by gallery staff around a theme, medium, style, or important historical moment; and those curated by individuals outside the gallery, whether that means a guest curator creating an exhibition for a host venue or a touring exhibition created by another gallery. To organize these exhibitions, gallery staff draw on their own experience and connections, but they also solicit proposals from artists and curators. This helps make the process more democratic. It also allows a gallery to tailor its programming to fit the needs of its community rather than the tastes, interests, and expertise of whoever happens to be running it.

While the AGN had continued to host exhibitions throughout its crisis, those exhibitions had not followed this model. This is not because the board and volunteers were uninterested in art; they were passionate about it and determined to keep the gallery alive. They were simply overwhelmed. There was no one who knew the collection, no clear parameters for determining which of the proposed exhibitions would be a good fit, and no money to pay the artists and curators who had proposed them if the gallery decided that they were. So the collection remained in the vault, the proposals in an ever-growing pile on the director's desk, and the walls hung with whatever the gallery's limited resources could manage—generally works for sale.

I began to reorient the AGN's programming to fit the regional public art gallery model I was familiar with, but I wanted to ensure our Northumberland community was well represented. For a small town, Cobourg is busy; people are out and about. Activities are plentiful, and alongside several active and well-attended, art-related groups there is a thriving local art scene. The community had supported the gallery through its worst, and it needed to anchor its revival. I also began to focus on the permanent collection and dedicated gallery space to presenting curated exhibitions of work the AGN owned. While it took a long time to move through and respond to all the exhibition proposals I had inherited, I know it was appreciated. Three of the submissions moved forward, and, after honoring the exhibitions that were already in place, the AGN had something that had for a long time seemed out of reach: a full schedule of programming that, by 2019, would see it looking like the engaged, vibrant public gallery it once was.

The sense of relief and excitement from the community that blossomed alongside the gallery was the best indication I could have hoped for that we were on the right track. From 2018 to the end of 2019, our attendance increased a whopping 250 percent. Northumberland County was rediscovering the AGN, and, in a way, the AGN was rediscovering Northumberland County. We began a Spotlight Series featuring local artists sharing their stories and passions for their art form, along with their personal connections to the local landscape and its people—intimate and interactive while building community collaborations. Exhibitions and events were well attended, and we were positioned to expand our education programs.

Sadly, in early 2020, COVID-19 closures and restrictions put us into a two-year holding pattern. We pivoted to online programming and were reminded that our most important asset was and remains our community. With community support, we persevered. While still in lockdown, we organized an exhibition and catalog that told the story of the AGN's first six decades through sixty works from its collection. We also welcomed the donation of 106 works, a generous private gift, and the start of a new era of acquisitions. By the end of 2021, the AGN was no longer in financial debt. The gallery emerged from the pandemic with two full-time and four part-time employees and forty volunteers—a remarkable achievement. We leveraged the financial support of our municipal partner to support successful applications for provincial and federal grants that will see the AGN into the next stage of its transformation.

None of these changes were easy. At times, tempers flared—the risks to the gallery were real, the prospect of losing it terrifying, and emotions ran high. Today, the working board that hired me and the volunteers who, warily at first, shared their stories about the gallery they were desperate to save are all gone. Board roles and responsibilities were clarified and replaced by a new, nonoperational board of passionate, enthusiastic volunteers who no longer have to carry the responsibility of running things day-to-day. Instead, the gallery has a patient, talented staff dedicated to making the AGN a community institution that brings art, imagination, and connection to all of Northumberland County. We are continuing to build connections to artists through studio visits and by soliciting exhibition proposals. The gallery itself—with a new wood floor and walls that are always freshly painted—presents a vibrant exhibition program and hosts public events including artist talks.

Collaborations with community groups and institutions have diversified the gallery's activities and drawn in new audiences. Essential to all this positive change are policies that clarify the gallery's mission and help keep everyone—staff, volunteers, the board—on the same page: a donations policy for soliciting and accepting gifts, governance documents, and updated bylaws that clarify the AGN's responsibilities to its stakeholders.

When I was deciding what I wanted my career to be, I wondered about becoming a teacher—I liked the idea of always learning and refining skills, including communication and leadership. Leading a public institution has given me exactly that, but until I arrived at the AGN, I wasn't aware of how important the role of educator was to the career I had chosen and to the kind of leader I had become. Art and culture enrich the lives of communities and individuals, but they are also specialized fields. Public galleries make them accessible. They provide context and a welcoming environment where people can ask questions about ideas or ways of representing ideas they might never have encountered before. But a gallery can't do that important work if it doesn't know how. This is what makes gallery leadership, or any kind of institutional leadership, so challenging. It is one thing to get your message out—to, in the gallery's case, educate the public about art. But, as I learned at the AGN, more challenging, and arguably more essential, is creating an environment where teaching and learning flow in all directions to support and strengthen an evolving mission. I used my experience to teach the AGN how to be a regional gallery again, and the AGN's community—its board and volunteers, local artists, collectors, and art lovers—taught me how to make it a regional gallery that would serve that community. The AGN team collaborated with me to make necessary but still terrifying changes, and their dedication gave me permission to let go of perfection and embrace uncertainty.

Today, the AGN is a welcoming space dedicated to connecting people with art. It continues to thrive. We are looking forward to the next steps in its transformation: building staff capacity, reaching financial stability for the short term and long term, refining organizational systems, and continuing to develop exciting and interesting programming. Since 2018, I have taught courses in finance and human resource management in a hospitality program at a local community college, passing on the management and leadership skills I learned at the RMG and AGN to a new generation. In parallel, the AGN has begun hosting six-month placements for new graduates funded by a government program to support young professionals. Not only has this given us extra hands to tackle projects like a much-needed audit of the collection, but it also serves a key part of our mission: building connections with a network of regional galleries across Canada. As the AGN's placement students move on to positions in larger institutions, they create links that help us align with and benefit from larger conversations about art galleries' purpose and responsibilities while providing them with a solid foundation that can meet the challenges in our ever-changing world.

Love and dedication—so essential to any nonprofit—kept the AGN alive through its crisis, but they were not enough to pull it out. The AGN needed to be focused and supported by experience, a clear mission, and the willingness to rebuild institutional knowledge from the ground up. I knew this going in. I did not know how challenging it would be to put these things in place, nor how meeting that challenge would not only strengthen my commitment to the essential role regional galleries play, but to the community that supports this gallery, that sustained it through its lowest point, and that has seen it through this transformation.

Sometimes, I think back to those early days at the AGN and marvel at the tenacity of my younger self. I remember clearly the heaviness in the pit of my stomach when I realized just how bad things were at my new home. That heaviness was quickly replaced by intense frustration at my inability to create change despite knowing exactly what needed to be done. I could have walked away—as other EDs did before me—but giving up simply isn't in my nature.

Through the moments of defeat and disappointment, I learned to accept things as they were. I also developed a new level of patience and an ability to manage my own expectations. I never accepted no as a final answer—I still don't—and I always found a way, maybe not the easy or direct way, but with perseverance came results.

I also learned to never underestimate the power of small wins—collectively, they make up huge steps forward.

During those early years, I leaned on two incredible women in the community who listened, supported, and encouraged me. They understood the situation and my need to process. Positive feedback from staff, board, volunteers, and the community encouraged the path forward. When you are well supported, you can achieve what may seem impossible.

Through this journey, the community has given me their trust, and I continue to work to ensure that both I and the AGN can keep it. Whether future changes require us to move slowly or at the speed of lightning, we've now built a foundation that will support the gallery for another sixty years and beyond.

❧ MEET THE AUTHORS ❧

MOJDEH COX

Mojdeh Cox is a dynamic leader known for uniting people to tackle complex issues through meaningful dialogue and actionable strategies. Over the past decade and a half, she has excelled in coaching leaders, businesses, and organizations across various sectors, guiding them to reimagine their work with an emphasis on equity and social justice.

Mojdeh's achievements are varied and significant. For example, she has organized the largest equity-based lobby on Parliament Hill for Indigenous rights with the Canadian Labour Congress and facilitated the co-creation of the Community Diversity and Inclusion Strategy for the City of London. Her engaging and relatable communication style makes her a sought-after speaker, writer, and media commentator on both national and international issues.

Her concept of Radical Accountability, developed during her tenure as a nonprofit president and CEO, has gained national recognition and become a part of the leadership and governance lexicon in the nonprofit sector. Mojdeh is also an award-winning consultant and convener. She founded Cox & Co., a full-scale, values-based consulting firm dedicated to building better institutions and thriving communities. Cox & Co specializes in ethical governance, organizational audits, and professional learning and development for leaders and their teams.

OLINDA CASIMIRO

Olinda Casimiro stands at the forefront of the cultural sector as the Executive Director of the Art Gallery of Northumberland in Cobourg, Ontario. With a remarkable 25 years of experience, she is a strategic thinker and a leader who is deeply inspired by the creative spirit of artists. Olinda's dedication to engaging communities through art has made a significant impact, particularly in presenting and interpreting artistic works that connect deeply with the public.

Her tenure has been marked by successfully raising funds for new programming and cultural initiatives in Cobourg and Northumberland County. Olinda's belief in the power of collaborative and diverse creative environments has driven substantial changes in the industry. Beyond her professional endeavors, Olinda is deeply rooted in community service, actively volunteering her time. An advocate for simplicity, she identifies as an aspiring minimalist, showcasing a keen interest in modern art. Alongside her role at the art gallery, Olinda imparts her wealth of knowledge as a professor at Durham College in Oshawa, contributing to the development of the next generation of leaders. Through her multifaceted engagement, Olinda Casimiro continues to weave a rich tapestry of creativity, community, and cultural enrichment.

Listen to the podcast episode!

REFLECTION QUESTIONS

1. Before you read this chapter, had you ever heard the term glass cliff assignment? What did it mean to you before reading the chapter? Has your understanding of the term changed after reading this chapter?

2. Mojdeh speaks honestly about her experience of being fired. One of the themes of her story is how she couldn't forgive herself for not noticing the "red flags" along the way. Has there been a time in your career when you noticed red flags? Did you say anything? Did you stay quiet and ignore them?

3. Do you think failure is an important component of leadership? Do you think the culture at your organization supports failure as part of the leadership journey?

4. When you are hired into a glass cliff assignment, there is so much that needs to change. If you were in charge, how would you introduce change? Quickly? Step-by-step? What would be most important to you as you led that process?

5. Olinda references in her story the women colleagues who were her support network during this challenging time at the gallery. Who would you lean on? Who could you ask for support on your leadership journey? What would change if you asked them to formally be on your "personal board of directors?"

VISIONARY

The ability to build a picture of a visionary future is a fundamental part of the identity of participants. It is more than just "something they do." The juxtaposition of vision, their role as a weather setter, and this hyperassociation with the organization creates a special ability for these leaders to extend the organization into the as-yet-unknown future.

COLLECTIVE VISION
by Heather Nelson

SITTING IN MY CAR outside the office of a national retailer, sweating.

This was it. This meeting had the potential to be game-changing for food security in this country, and I knew it in my heart. I could not mess this up. I'd done my research and knew this company had invested big in the charitable sector before and the possibilities were huge.

Did I mention I was sweating? And also, I had mistakenly worn a top where you could see the flush already climbing up my neck. Damn the face blush that has been giving away my feelings since I was old enough to have any!

I was in a new role as the head of fundraising for a national food security organization. I had just returned from maternity leave and was wondering if I'd lost the skills it took to make anything happen other than a stealth diaper change, and here I was walking into a huge company with deep pockets trying to secure a big donation.

Maybe I was meant to stay home a bit longer?

Did I want it too badly?

This could be the corporate donation that set me up for success.

I was told visualization was supposed to help in these situations.

Sitting in my car, I started picturing the person I was going to meet. Definitely a power broker in the company. A tall, suit-wearing, blunt negotiator. I bet he'd be abrupt and determined to get more than he gave. Wasn't this how it worked with companies and charities?

At this stage in my career, corporate partnerships between charities and companies were so new to me. I had led one super successful one at a previous job, had a business degree, and had read all the books. None of that was going to help me today. I really didn't have enough experience to know exactly how this sort of partnership could come together.

What I knew is that my charity had value. I believed that any partnership needed to benefit both organizations. It needed to meet the mission of my charity and the goals of the business.

I knew all of that but would I be able to get the message across as effectively as I needed to? Would I be able to stick with it when pushed? I didn't know. I had never had a meeting this important. Why didn't I ease in with something smaller?

As I walked into the building, I was definitely picturing some version of Gordon Gekko from the *Wall Street* movie slamming his hand on the desk and asking for everything as I skulked out of their office with the worst deal ever for my charity.

In a dingy room with yellow walls and fluorescent lighting, I sat on a plastic chair and stared at a blank whiteboard and waited for Mark to enter.

I had talked to others on my team before taking this meeting and there were definitely mixed opinions on whether this company was the right national partner. I believed that this partnership could be a huge financial win for my organization, its mission, *and* for my fundraising objectives. It would be the very best way to establish myself in my new role.

Mark walked in totally relaxed, wearing a blue shirt, sleeves rolled up, with a gentle accent and smile.

Sitting across from me, he was warm and disarming.

Not Gordon Gekko. Not the person I had pictured.

Someone who wanted to talk, learn, and share. My intimidation washed away, and we got down to business.

Mark had done this before, he explained. "We are a national retailer and want to give food to food banks all across the country, wherever there is a store. We know we have the infrastructure to do this, but Canada is big. There are local issues to consider and we want to work with an organization that can make this happen with us."

My excitement mounted. I could see it now. The financial investment in my organization and the positive impact on food banks all across the country—it would meet both of my objectives. The path to success immediately started forming in my mind. I could lead this project. I could make this happen.

We talked about what was possible now and in the future. As we mapped out the possibilities, I could only see all the ways this was going to work. I talked faster and got more excited.

My vision started to form. My national food security charity would be the lead national charitable partner for this retailer. Every store would be matched to a food bank. Food and money would flow from stores to the food banks. More food and money to food banks and ultimately to people all across the country.

I'd secure enough funding nationally for my organization to lead this program and start a new way of working between a national retailer and the food bank community.

I knew Mark believed it too. He was going to be my partner in achieving it.

After the meeting, driving to my office while blasting loud music, I pictured the celebration when I told everyone about the funding, the food, and the big opportunity. I had already secured a significant financial donation to my organization and it was just the beginning.

I arrived back at the office. So excited. So proud of myself. So relieved.

I'd done it. I'd raised money. I'd started to build a relationship with a company with huge potential.

Knocking on my executive director's office door, beaming, I said, "The meeting was great, and I closed one hundred thousand dollars in support! Don't worry though—that is just the beginning. This is going to be huge. Millions!"

After expressing her congratulations, she immediately brought my other senior team members into the conversation—our programming and marketing leads. They did not join the celebration. They both began to share their concerns. They could see so many challenges. Their excitement of my big win was very muted.

My stomach dropped. I left her office. So disappointed. The smooth and easy road to my vision was not shared. My excitement was not contagious. I was sullen as I drove home.

Over the coming weeks, I tried to figure out how I could bring my vision to life.

I pondered so many scenarios. I tried to figure out how I could somehow do the majority of the work on my own, with my own team. This was clearly impossible. To do so would greatly limit the scope of the project and probably disappoint my corporate partner. However, while I knew it was impossible, the temptation to hold on tight to the vision, develop and protect it, and control as much as possible was strong. I wanted this project and partnership to be successful so badly. Yet, I had neither the knowledge, the power, nor the influence to do it alone no matter how much I might have wished that was the case.

I was the new team member. Everyone else on the management team had more direct experience in national program execution than I did. I was a fundraiser. My experience was in relationship building, raising money, and figuring out the charity-company alignment. While it wasn't going to be easy, the partnership was in my wheelhouse, and I was ready for the persistent and creative pursuit of a strong partnership that was going to be required.

However, it was the rest of the team, and people beyond my organization, who had developed initiatives of this size and scope. Even with my best negotiation skills and the very best partnership in place, I needed a team of people to execute against what I was promising the national retailer we were going to do. I started to feel very underequipped to make this opportunity come to fruition.

Working in my office, I carefully planned the meeting to share my plan with the management team. While I wanted the big idea right away, I knew that would never work. I had to figure out how to bring them and their knowledge into my vision. They were the most important people in making the project happen successfully. It's not that they didn't want it to happen, they did, but it was going to impact them differently and they had a wider view of the stakeholders. For me, getting the investment in place and establishing the corporate partnership was the hard part; for them there was going to be a lot of change and a lot of work. So despite my desire to get to my end goal as quickly as possible, I scaled back my early ideas. I tried hard to prepare for the points of view of others.

This was going to be a journey, not a sprint, and a real test of my patience.

I set the meeting in the morning, my best time and hopefully when others were fresh. I gave us lots of time. I had scaled back my initial objective to focus on getting their commitment to a pilot project.

The pilot would mean starting with pairing a group of food banks with a group of stores to execute the food getting from stores to food banks. The engagement of customers and marketing would need to wait for the next phase of expansion. I needed to get the internal team to say yes to the pilot project and to lead the strategy to get food banks on board.

My executive director, marketing lead, program lead, and myself all joined the meeting. My objective: to get their buy-in, understand their perspectives, and leverage their knowledge.

I agonized over a carefully worded briefing memo and thoughtful agenda I sent. I set my intention: I was determined to listen.

No sooner than a few minutes into the conversation . . .

Program Lead: I'm pretty sure quite a few food banks already have this program in place locally. We should just let it be.

Marketing Lead: Well, it's really unclear how the logistics are going to work. We need to ensure that there are tight controls on the food donated. We also need to consider that there are so many different sizes of food banks, and some don't have enough trucks already. How are they going to respond?

Marketing Lead: Is there an opportunity to do this program without an accompanying marketing campaign?

Program Lead: Maybe we could test the idea with one or two food banks in Ontario. A year-one strategy to gradually see where the challenges will be.

I was listening, and I could hear the obstacles stacking up. I was starting to panic. I began to picture having to go back to Mark and to tell him that all I could make happen was a pilot with two food banks. I could not imagine selling that as a big enough first step.

My heart was beating fast. I couldn't lose this opportunity. A pilot that really wasn't extensive would be hard to explain to Mark even though he was kind and supportive. I needed to establish that we were truly committed to the size and scope of the program that made sense for a national retailer. I was determined to demonstrate that we were the partner that could fulfill the retailer's expectations.

After much discussion, a compromise was reached and a substantial pilot agreed to. It was the first step, and with the management team onside growing the group of people needed to make the project happen, it was going to be easier. I'd passed the first big test on the road to making this project a reality. We were moving forward.

Coming out of the meeting, and through subsequent conversations, I began to understand how much opportunity there was for me to learn, and for the project to build with the management team's expertise. I started to accept—perhaps a bit reluctantly— that learning from them would require a slower and scaled-back approach than I'd originally imagined.

Despite these adjustments, my optimism and belief in myself and vision did not waver, and I began to adjust my vision and the plan to make it happen.

With the pilot underway, I increasingly appreciated the value of the perspective of others. It was the right decision to start this way and learn. This approach also gave me the time to build more allies. I shifted focus to ways to bring others into evolving the vision of success.

Over a period of several years, there were many meetings, often with me pushing for big and bold action and others recommending a more conservative approach. As the project moved forward, I gathered information and understanding.

I worked alongside more team members and more food banks to build pilot projects and to test different approaches. Year over year, new elements were added to the program, elements that broadened the scope, made the project more effective, and improved the results on both sides of the partnership. Through the input of others, my vision became a collective vision and the partnership, and its impact on food security, continued to grow and evolve.

With the national retailer, I was focused on strengthening the relationship and increasing the investment in both our national and local operations. I had regular meetings to update Mark and his colleagues on our progress. I clipped newspaper articles to suggest new ideas I thought we could implement and sent them over to Mark's office. We jointly solved emerging challenges and came up with ways of including employees and customers in the project's expansion. A true partnership formed.

In hindsight, it is easy for me to see now that there were more supporters than I believed at the time. It's easier for me to recognize that my excitement and commitment to the vision led to me seeing people that were providing challenges and potential solutions as obstacles. It's easier for me to acknowledge that as I shifted that perspective to one of gathering allies and valuing their input, the program built and grew.

Most importantly, as I embraced the idea that I could be the champion of the vision and also allow it to evolve with other experts leading it as well, the impact would be bigger and more significant. By listening to others, different paths to success emerged, and we followed different opportunities than I had originally considered. All along I had believed in the opportunity and as more leaders and supporters joined—some with even more lofty goals than I had—we were able to have a greater joint impact than I had anticipated.

Several years after that first meeting, a collective approach to implementing the program was in place and ultimately, our collective vision was realized: a retailer partnership that was nationwide and combined food and funding getting to food banks along with a high-profile marketing campaign. The growing partnership was meeting our national goal of increased food and funding to local food banks while also providing us with national support to execute the program. The company was meeting their objectives of getting food to people who needed it while engaging their customers and employees. The partnership was established and flourishing despite the bumps along the way. A new way of partnering with retailers was underway. It was a partnership that I was proud of.

I hope you aren't reading this and thinking that holding on tight to a vision isn't the way to go. *It is!*

I still believe passionately that had I not held this vision, things would have happened in a very different way. Does that mean it wouldn't have still happened—of course not. Others would have carried it forward. However, in this timeline, in this way, my vision was important.

That, however, is only part of the story, as my vision alone was not enough. I needed others and their knowledge. I needed their experience. I needed their hard work. It was through their commitment to the project that my vision became our vision. The opportunity evolved and grew well beyond where it began. A community of people emerged to bring the vision to fruition. I consider this the real success of my leadership story.

Today, I run my own consulting business, focused on supporting charities in building partnerships with companies. With BridgeRaise, I hold on tight to the vision that the world is a better place thanks to the important role that companies play in partnership with charities. This collective vision is held by my clients, my team, and my community.

The lesson I'd like to share with you is this: As a leader, find and hold a vision that is important to you. Allow yourself to enjoy the energy and excitement that comes from that initial spark of a new idea. It is such an awesome and powerful feeling.

As you move from idea to vision to plan, notice all the opportunities to include others. Listen to them and allow them to become a part of the evolution of the vision and the implementation of the plan. Build the community that will achieve the impact together.

This is your true measure of success.

NOW WHAT?
by Carley Scheck

SEPTEMBER 2020, five months into the pandemic.

My business partner (who also happens to be my husband) came to me and laid out a very clear, very detailed report. This forecast demonstrated in painstaking detail the financial implications of continuing to operate our venue and cooking school, both of which relied on hosting in-person culinary events and gatherings. This was a true "home" that we had invested sixteen years in building. And now, this home was in jeopardy.

Normally, in my line of business, you are well prepared for fallout. This is the epitome of the events industry: anything and everything could—and does—go wrong. Our team is always prepared with contingency plans. You always have a Plan B, Plan C, Plan D . . . and when all else fails, you wing it. Never before in my business career had I felt so incredibly unprepared.

I recall exactly what room I was in when my husband showed me the forecasts. In an instant, I felt the ground beneath me evaporate. I watched from above as my body dealt with the blow of this life-altering news. A million thoughts rushed through my head, fighting for attention:

What does this mean for our family?

What about our loyal team?
Can we afford to keep anyone?
What will our employees do?
What about their families?
Where will our people celebrate and gather?
How can we close our doors?
How can we not?

It was hard to swallow that our beloved venue, the space that united so many incredible people—employees, clients, and guests—would never be filled again. Our team was a close-knit and like-minded group, and it was our mission to help people celebrate life's mile markers. Weddings, birthdays, anniversaries, and other milestones were celebrated within those walls. Many clients moved beyond regulars and loyal brand ambassadors to become extensions of our work family.

Truly, this space was a home away from home. I had become so intimately entwined with my role that I will admit it was part of my identity. Imagine someone telling you that you could no longer be who you felt you were, in the home you had created. It was deeply personal.

The notion of closing the business entirely was not an option. But I was forced to make the difficult decision to close our physical space. As tough as that decision was, communicating the news to the team was worse. As I reviewed with them the permanent changes we needed to make and our plan for vacating the building, they remained gracious and understanding.

We modified the business model almost overnight from a physical venue to an online operation. Between all the organizing and packing, we were simultaneously running what was now an online cooking school, while constantly modifying our formula to work within the parameters of an ever-changing world. We had gone from full control of our own space to no control.

There developed a sort of "in it together" mentality that unified the remaining team in incredible ways, but it was debilitating for a small team to carry such a big load for so long. Meanwhile, I felt incredibly isolated and untethered, and things were moving so quickly that I barely had a moment to acknowledge the grief that I was feeling.

As the CEO, I had always held the honing rod for the company vision. Now, I was tasked with navigating our future with a completely new business model and no idea what the next six months of the pandemic would bring. I was constantly turning over a single question in my head: *Now what?*

Short-term solutions were easy in the way that survival is easy: straightforward, one foot in front of the other, solve for the immediate threat. But crafting a strategic response to the ever-changing business environment during and post-pandemic required longer-term planning. There were no clear answers. There was so much change happening so quickly, and I was fully immersed in the day-to-day operations, unable to get out of the business minutia. Normally, entrepreneurs find change exciting and invigorating, but this period left me feeling tremendously unsettled.

In my earlier years of management, I received positive reinforcement for my boots-on-the-ground approach to leadership, which ultimately shaped my personal leadership style and is now woven into the fabric of my own business. I became known as the person who worked alongside staff and contributed wherever was needed. That meant setting the tables and polishing the cutlery; working services and closing the late nights; hitting the ground running alongside my team. It also meant contingency planning and troubleshooting and people looking to me for the way out and the way forward. I was still their leader, but I did it from the ground up. I was comfortable being that "doer" because it helped me feel in control and as an extrovert, I was energized by personal interactions.

Leading this way has its benefits. The trust established early on between me and our team remains an important differentiator in the business, where people are a key component of our value proposition. Team members know that I will set them up for success and ensure that they have tools and support systems at their disposal so they can be at their best. As a result, we built an extremely loyal and close-knit team, one with shared values and a culture of contribution.

As you can imagine, delegation doesn't come naturally to me. I had to learn to put the right people in the right roles and then trust them to do their jobs while on maternity leave. That distance from the day-to-day operations forced me to shift from the "doer" role to the "weather setter" role. My team didn't need me running the minutia, they needed me to set the direction of the company and steer the ship.

Over time, I developed a supportive team, with people in the right places, all driven by a shared mission and annual growth. The combined strengths of my management team meant that I could focus on my visionary role: overseeing business development opportunities, setting strategy and direction, and even pursuing professional growth outside of my own company.

I was able to take on new projects that were challenging and stretchy but aligned with my personal mission and goals. I began teaching business classes at the local college and co-created a food literacy program for schools. This work was uplifting, fulfilling, and invigorating. I also found it to be very complementary to my role as CEO, helping me tap into an even greater capacity for leadership.

And then the pandemic hit. And we were down employees, and my whole world tilted on an axis. The years that followed were bumpy and full of trial and error. Our industry was rocked with some of its biggest challenges ever, with unprecedented labor shortages, skyrocketing food costs, supply chain breakdowns, and employees getting sick for long stretches of time.

My team needed my on-the-ground leadership to create stability and support the work that needed to be done. The business needed my visionary leadership to set a direction and guide the strategy to get there. The struggle to be both an on-the-ground leader and a visionary leader were in true conflict. I was so *in it* that I didn't even have time to consider which approach was right or wrong. I was just doing whatever needed to be done.

By 2022 the resilience I had worn as an armor was wearing thin. The constant mental battle of "in" the business versus "visionary leader" was slowing me down. I was constantly context switching to juggle both roles. I put an enormous amount of pressure on myself to figure it all out and insisted on bearing the burden alone, despite my husband's overtures of support.

My attempt to be on top of it all ultimately compromised my mental and physical health. In the aftermath, I found myself replacing "Now what?" with a new question: *What do I need?* After all, isn't it my responsibility to ensure I have the energy, resilience, and focus to guide my organization through the next set of challenges? I posed this question to my business coach. As a good coach would do, he did not provide the answer. Rather, he invited me to sink into reflection.

I had almost forgotten what it felt like to tap into my own intuition, that inner knowing that had guided me through so many tough decisions over the years. In some ways, I'd considered my intuition a superpower. But I had pushed down this all-knowing as I willed my way through the pandemic. Now, I took a break from the business, got quiet, and put pen to paper.

Below you'll find an excerpt from that moment of honesty and clarity. Rereading it now, I see it as a love letter to myself and a renewed commitment to following the lead of my inner wisdom:

The path that I am currently on is directly affecting my ability to see hope and, ultimately, move forward.

This is keeping me feeling "stuck."

I acknowledge that my role truly IS the big picture leader in the company. And that what I am doing now and where I am now, is not congruent with this role.

I have forgotten that this is innately who I am, who I have developed into over the years. This is where I feel utterly and truly at home.

The current operational minutia is affecting that big picture connection that I thrive on—it is affecting my drive and creativity, which I need to feel personally and professionally fulfilled.

And leadership—I am not being an effective leader by drowning in the minutia.

I need to move out of this operational minutia as best I can now, or at least begin the process of the transition. To get back to all the areas that align with my desire to innovate and foster creativity again, and to move back to the core of why I am here in the first place: the desire to build something of value and impact. It is my gift to continually offer something inspiring and motivating for my team—for all the reasons why we do what we do.

I have been so resistant and reluctant to challenge these feelings (or perhaps not been able to articulate these feelings thus far?). I have resisted these feelings for the practicality of the rebuild, or for the notion of having to work IN all the roles to best understand them (and that becoming a default I can't untangle), or for the self-sacrificing belief of having to shoulder it all. I have acted as if I have no choice—but I have clearly forgotten. I do have a choice.

I emerged from this break with a commitment to step back and seek ways to reorganize the operation. This included implementing some new tools and support systems and hiring more high-level team members. Even with this renewed knowledge, investment, and my commitment to put processes in place, the reality of the business environment in which we were operating continued to be dynamic. I continued to be pulled in many directions.

There exists a fine line between leadership and management. There can even be tension between the two. What is clear is that both can serve businesses and organizations in distinct ways. I imagine that a corporate CEO might have a better chance of creating a clear distinction thanks to the more formal structures created within an organization. By contrast, an entrepreneurial

CEO might have a more complex and layered experience because of the personal and financial stakes at risk.

Can the merging of these two entities—manager and visionary—exist? Perhaps. I am still not sure. For me, the art of being a leader is knowing when to step in and knowing when to step back. The willingness to get on the ground is a necessary part of business survival, but what I also am learning is that it is not necessary to be just one or the other: the manager or the CEO. Different businesses need different approaches. My growth will continue as I adapt to living in both of these roles. I now see this fluidity as a unique aspect of our company and, quite frankly, as a differentiator for myself as a leader.

Entrepreneurship requires you to go where the business needs you. I think this has also contributed to some of the inner conflict I've experienced as a visionary leader in trying to figure out "the right way" to lead. As an entrepreneur, I really do wear many hats. One day I could be washing dishes, and the next I am strategizing and negotiating collaborative partnerships and seeking additional growth opportunities. The "right way" may never exist, nor be a reality in my world. The notion of leading in a certain way, or the way someone has a vision of you leading, can create so much conflict and negativity.

Today, I choose leadership that upholds authenticity and vulnerability. Authenticity allows me the freedom to know I can choose where and when I show up. Vulnerability means I accept the fact that there can be a risk to this approach and that if the line is blurred too much, there could be a tipping point. There are times when I think: *Could I be further along if I did things differently or "acted" more like a CEO—if I got stronger about boundaries, if*

I mastered time management, if I delegated more? Perhaps. But I am learning to embrace the fact that the kind of visionary leader our particular business needs is one who is both standing in the forest and well above it. Big picture and small details.

I am living so many of these exact experiences and feelings as I write this chapter. The lessons learned here are not so much reflective of experiences of events that have come and gone, but ones that I am living in the moment. When I come home from a particularly intense day and digest the takeaways, I am reminded: *I am okay with the way I am leading.*

I am on this journey to be the leader I choose to be, and my organization will benefit. I am giving myself permission to step outside this rigid definition and letting go of the notion that I must be one or the other. I also recognize that our business is currently in another growth stage. This calls for different strategies and approaches.

I have been invited into this recent understanding as I live through the experiences of trying to balance the two constraints— the manager and the leader. I now recognize that the internal discontent I feel comes from a liminal space—the middle space— which is neither here nor there. I acknowledge this as I write this chapter. I am processing this and realizing that I can reject the idea that it must be one or the other. Leadership is complex, and for me, it is deeply personal. My business is a manifestation of myself, after all.

For now, my commitment is this: to continue the journey forward as the manager, the entrepreneur, and the visionary CEO. My story and my chapter continue to be written.

NO RIGHT WAY
by Jenny Mitchell

YOUR BODY DOESN'T KNOW how to lie. But your brain sure does!

The wackiness in my body started innocently enough: I would feel lightheaded every once in a while, and I'd have trouble catching my breath at random moments of the day. At first, I dismissed them as one-offs.

But then, in the spring of 2018, these incidents started getting worse. Consistently worse. By the time I had finally given in and labeled them panic attacks, they were happening regularly and, worst of all, I had no idea when they would arrive. They seemed to have no rhyme or reason . . . or so I told myself.

There was nothing out of the ordinary on the day of this particular panic attack. I was coming back from the gym, on a familiar route. Out of the blue, my chest started to feel constricted, and I suddenly felt dizzy. Again.

And here I am, driving down Lancaster Road in Ottawa, about to pass out!

Oh, the irony, dear reader. In the middle of having a panic attack, Jenny Mitchell's logical brain takes over and says, "Jenny. You don't want to pass out driving a car. Get yourself to a public space. Now. Make haste!"

The grocery store was not an option. No place to sit there. But the bank would have seats, right? I could be inconspicuous while I caught my breath and avoided fainting. I parked and walked into the RBC Bank and sat down on the dirty green couch. Another logical thought: *If I did end up passing out, at least someone would be there to see me fall.*

My body was trying to tell me something, but I was too busy—or too proud—to listen. What I came to realize later was that these attacks were linked to the decision I had made to take on a new volunteer leadership position as chair of the board of directors at my local tennis club. And I was struggling with the "right" way to do leadership.

On paper, I was the right person to lead the board of directors. I had read all the books about leadership and had coached hundreds of leaders as part of my work as an executive coach.

That is one of my big takeaways about the process of stepping in to become a leader: there is a big difference between textbook leadership and the reality of messy, complex, imperfect leadership.

I would figure this all out much later.

I had joined the board of the tennis club four years earlier. The word *board* conjures up for me all sorts of images of imposing people sitting around a large—preferably wooden!—table. This was a place that held power, a place where change could take place. Equal parts fear and excitement coursed through my veins. Everyone was older than me (not unusual), and I was determined to make my contribution at this table count. I was determined to get it right, whatever "getting it right" meant.

In 2018, I became president of the board of directors at a club where only one other woman had held that position in the club's 136-year history. There had been years of infighting at the membership-based organization—a tennis club that had been in existence since 1881. The legal constraints of the existing governance structure—where the people that held substantial power to make decisions were no longer active members of the club—had stifled the natural process of organizational evolution and change.

The world had literally evolved around the club. While the club had originally been set up as a private club on the outskirts of Ottawa, the city had grown, and the club now occupied five acres of prime land in the heart of downtown. Natural evolution had also been stifled by a fundamental governance decision dating back to 1939. The club operated as a not-for-profit in every way except one: rather than voting members, the club had shareholders as you would have at a for-profit corporation like, say, Bell Canada.

The challenge of every single board of directors from the last sixty years had been how to make decisions while living under the shadow of a group of shareholders for whom the club and its assets were just a potential "cash cow" when it was sold.

The club was frozen in time, waiting for the moment it would either be forced to change or go bankrupt. The century-old clubhouse was falling down, the club had a hard time recruiting board members (because who takes on a volunteer role to be yelled at?), and the financial balance sheet was in shambles.

The change came in the form of the Ontario government. The government rolled out new legislation for not-for-profits. And in it, they decreed that not-for-profit entities in Ontario could no longer hold governance structures with shares.

The club was going to have to amend its bylaws in order to comply. And to amend the bylaws, the club was going to have to have two-thirds of current shareholders vote in favor of abolishing their own shares. The people who voted on club business would no longer be shareholders, they would be voting members, as per the newly proposed bylaws.

It took not one, not two, but three attempts to pass the new bylaws.

And this, dear reader, is where I walked in as chair of the board, two months after this historic transition took place.

We finally had the opportunity to create change and the pressure was on me to lead. I'd better do this the right way.

Every chair of the board had contributed something over their leadership tenure: one had gotten rid of the twenty-six lawn bowlers who were a massive drain on the balance sheet as compared to the 470 active tennis players. One had cleaned up the balance sheet, raised fees to align with inflation, and paid down debt. And my predecessor had successfully transitioned the organization into a full not-for-profit organization.

Into these big shoes I stepped, with my chin held high, determined to lead just like them.

And that was exactly the problem. These former chairs were *not* like me. But I tried to make that style work.

During those first few months as chair, I took everything on my own shoulders. I avoided asking for help because I thought that would show weakness. The waves of self-doubt washed over me regularly, and I would compensate by overpreparing for board meetings: If this happens, I'll do this. If we go here, I'll move there.

Catastrophizing. Defending. Finding ways to protect myself from others finding out that I was floundering.

I remember feeling very exposed, like I was in a spotlight, and that everyone was watching me. When I scanned my past experiences with leadership and leaders, the models I knew were so boxy, authoritative, and unwavering. The women leaders I knew were more Angela Merkel or Hillary Clinton—electable women because of their strong masculine energy. I knew there had to be another way to lead. I was searching for it, and I knew that it was out there, but it wasn't clear yet.

I couldn't do it. I tried very hard—because I am an achiever—to lead like other people. My body was rebelling while my mind was still trying to make it work.

At the intersection of fear, anxiety, self-doubt, and expectations sat my panic attack. I had stepped into this vortex of behaviors that felt wrong, and my body was telling me, "Danger, danger! Retreat immediately!"

Did others notice?

With the gift of hindsight, I can tell you that no one was watching. That was my ego talking, telling me not to mess up or I would be in big trouble. I had an expectation of what leadership was supposed to look and feel like. That decision would be clearer once I was in charge. That if I showed vulnerability, people would think I was unqualified. That if I didn't know the answer, people wouldn't trust me.

You're never really "ready" to lead. The opportunity presents itself and you either step up, or you don't. I had this assumption that the way I was most comfortable leading was not acceptable. Not "right" enough.

It's really quite amazing how much planning you can do in the pursuit of "not looking stupid." I had this belief that the entire future of this organization rested on my shoulders, and I needed to "figure this out."

Why wasn't my collaborative, people-focused, heart-centered approach enough?

My body knew. I knew I had to stop trying to fit into some version of a leader I was not.

I turned to my leadership books. All the textbooks said that organizations should do strategic planning. So I engaged a facilitator to lead us through the process.

We were not ready to talk about our future vision of the organization. We were essentially a two-month-old organization that had taken over a hundred years to be birthed. I noticed a huge cultural disconnect happening: the facilitator was talking about building the club for the future, and board members were reluctant to give up the conversation about weeds on the courts. They weren't ready to see the future. They had to get comfortable with who they had just become. It was too soon. But I had trusted the books over my own judgment.

With the wisdom of leadership experience and reflection, I can see that I felt personally responsible for the success of that planning session. No one asked me to. I just assumed that that was what being a number one was about.

When I came home from the strategic planning session, I told my husband all about it (because I always seek out sounding boards, and he's the best one I know). I had to let go of "doing leadership the right way." I had to start figuring out what Jenny's right way was because the other way was literally sending me into panic attacks.

One of the most powerful things to say out loud is, "I feel like we are at a crossroads. Where do we go from here?" That's how I wanted to lead.

What the leadership books don't tell you is that you have to breathe life into your style of leadership. That the most important part of leading is, well, you. And liking you, liking how you lead, and being vulnerable enough to seek out feedback from others is a fundamental ingredient.

You have to trust yourself and give yourself permission to embrace your strengths and acknowledge your gaps, all while asking for help from others to fill the voids. As much as I was in charge, I couldn't do this alone. And my sounding board was my peers: my eight peers around the board table. We were a team.

Did my peers notice how I was grappling with leading? I remember working in a coffee shop in my neighborhood and just by chance, my VP on the board came by and sat down to say hello. The first thing he said was, "You seem stressed. How are you?" I immediately teared up because, yes, he had noticed.

Some people call it confidence; I prefer to think of it as reframing your relationship with self-doubt. The doubt is not going away, but over time and with experience, that voice of self-doubt becomes a little bit softer, a little bit less of a bully in your head. I have spoken to many women leaders about this experience. Whether it's social conditioning, or how we grew up, many women struggle with speaking their own truth without that niggling self-doubt. My working theory is that everyone has it, but some people choose to acknowledge the voice and then make the decision to step through the discomfort anyway. That's what confidence is. A deep level of "knowing" of yourself and your own potential. Because, dear reader, no one is exactly like you!

I wish I could wrap this story up with a bow and say that from then on it was smooth sailing and I was able to let go of my mantra of "getting it right." That would make a much better ending. But life is not like a Disney princess movie.

In small ways, I began infusing my leadership style with me: making more space for discussion and dialogue; thinking of board meetings as collaborations, not just meetings once a month; and spending time building trust with each of the members of our board so that I could facilitate the partnership on our shared journey—not my journey, but rather our collective journey.

Leadership experiences change you. When I look at the pillars of Dr. Rehbein's research, I identify the most with being a visionary leader. It's been a consistent thread in my personal leadership narrative. In fact, I remember my father saying to me one time, "If it wasn't difficult, you wouldn't be interested, Jenny!" What I hope to do going forward is to add in self-reflection as a cornerstone of my work. I need time to think about how I choose to lead.

How have I been changed by my experiences?

Today, I no longer expend copious amounts of energy trying to get things right or trying to lead in a certain way. I am keenly aware of my strengths and limitations, and I focus my energy on uplifting and empowering the people around me. While I still prepare for important meetings, I know that it is more important to be present than to be right. And I trust that as long as I come in with an open heart and good intentions, I have confidence in my ability to address any challenges that may come up.

The shift in my leadership style gives the people I work with the permission they need to thrive, try new things, and explore their roles, without the looming fear of failure.

I trust myself. And because I trust myself, I can trust them.

And what is the right way to lead, anyway?

Trying to lead the "right way" and modeling other people's styles robbed me of my confidence. It took a physical manifestation of this lack of alignment for me to face what was going on. The minute I understood that the immense pressure I was putting on myself was not only unrealistic but also unhelpful in the pursuit of my goal, the panic attacks stopped. I was able to lead from a place of my confidence and knowledge.

The corporate world has a built-in hierarchy where "she/he who is your boss is always right." This is not true. The older I get, the more "gray" the world is. (Some days I long for my twenty-five-year-old self's view of the world that was so much more black and white). There is nuance and strategy in just about every decision you make. Your job as a leader is to make sure *you* and your ego are not getting in the way of making a great decision for your organization. The more you know yourself and your potential blind spots, the more effective you will be. That's where I focus my energy these days. And as an executive coach, I have the privilege of sitting in partnership with my clients to discover their true selves and their blind spots so they can lead in their own way too.

Self-assessment and personal reflection are hard work. I avoided it for years. Give yourself grace, stop being so hard on yourself, and learn how to celebrate how *you* do you. You don't have to do this alone.

It is *so* much better on this side of the story.

Would you rather lead the right way, or be confident leading your own way?

The choice is up to you.

⤍ MEET THE AUTHORS ⤏

HEATHER NELSON, MBA, CFRE

Heather Nelson, MBA, CFRE, is the founder and president of BridgeRaise, a boutique fundraising consultancy. With her team, Heather specializes in helping nonprofits enhance their fundraising efforts by forging corporate partnerships based on aligned values. Under her leadership, BridgeRaise has significantly influenced the nonprofit sector, assisting hundreds of charities in establishing meaningful corporate relationships over the past eight years.

With a career entirely dedicated to the nonprofit sector, Heather's expertise spans program management, marketing, and fundraising. Notably, she was the pioneering fundraiser at Food Banks Canada where she developed and expanded the corporate partnership program into a multi-million-dollar endeavor.

In addition to her professional achievements, Heather is a passionate mentor and educator. She has taught Introduction to Fundraising at Toronto Metropolitan University and is an active member of AFP Golden Horseshoe. Beyond her professional life, Heather enjoys the serenity of nature, spending time with her dog, and embracing the joys of being a hockey mom. She is also an avid LinkedIn user where she actively engages with the broader community.

CARLEY SCHELCK

Carley Schelck, the passionate owner and CEO of The Urban Element, infuses her work with a lively spirit and a profound love for the culinary world. Since founding the Ottawa-based boutique culinary experiences and event management company in 2005, Carley has become renowned for her infectious enthusiasm and meticulous attention to detail.

Her zeal for the culinary arts extends into the community, where she champions greater access to food and food education. This dedication birthed Cultivating Cooks, an innovative classroom-based program that equips youth with essential life skills, like growing and cooking their own food. Committed to the principle of lifelong learning, Carley places a strong emphasis on education in both her professional journey and personal growth.

As a teacher in the School of Business at Algonquin College, she guides graduates transitioning into the business world, sharing her experiences and insights. Carley's entrepreneurial spirit shines through as she navigates the challenges of business with unwavering optimism and a keen eye for opportunity.

JENNY MITCHELL, CFRE, CEC, DMA

Jenny Mitchell, a dynamic speaker, executive coach, podcaster, and professional fundraiser, is driven by a passion for inspiring excellence in others. Her podcast, "Underdog Leadership," focuses on empowering individuals to ascend professionally and personally. Jenny's influence extends to hundreds of CEOs, executive directors, and board members across Canada, assisting them in raising millions for charitable causes. Her client list includes notable organizations like the McMichael Canadian Art Collection, the University of Ottawa, and Queen's University.

Jenny completed her executive coaching training at Royal Roads University with a clear purpose: to enable ambitious and compassionate women leaders to embrace and own their unique leadership styles. Her personal mission is to engage in meaningful conversations that empower others to fully utilize their seat at the table.

Through her company, Chavender, Jenny is committed to nurturing the next generation of leaders through executive and group coaching, mastermind programs, and talent development initiatives. Recently, she has expanded her expertise to for-profit corporations and is a certified Enneagram iEQ9 Practitioner, enhancing her ability to conduct team workshops and professional growth sessions.

Listen to the podcast episode!

REFLECTION QUESTIONS

1. When you can see a vision for the future, and others cannot, what are the steps that you use to bring them along in your journey?

2. Heather talks about her experience of building more allies for her vision for the corporate partnership that she confirmed. Who are your allies at work? How do you cultivate these relationships on an ongoing basis?

3. One element of Heather's story is the idea of including people in the vision, moving from a personal vision to a collective vision for success. This requires letting go of some control to bring new ideas into the conversation. How comfortable are you with this approach? Is this a natural gift for you, or is this something you'd like to get better at as a leader?

4. Carley talks about her pride in being a "boots-on-the-ground" leader. But she also contrasts that with her desire to be visionary—to dream and to create. Do you feel that same push and pull? Which leadership style do you identify with from Carley's story? Why?

5. What do you think is the difference between the manager and the visionary? Do you think they can coexist? How would you make that happen?

6. Jenny's story describes how she was physically crippled by panic attacks trying to do leadership the "right way." Do you feel that same pressure to lead the right way? Have you ever had physical manifestations of your stress or anxiety about leading?

7. Who are your role models for empathetic and ambitious women leaders? Who inspires you?

ABOUT THE AUTHORS

In the Spring of 2023, twelve remarkable women leaders converged in Toronto, united by a shared vision to illuminate the diverse experiences of leadership for the next generation of women leaders. This gathering brought together trailblazers from various sectors—nonprofit leadership, healthcare philanthropy, arts and culture management, education, corporate strategy, and more. Each woman, an accomplished figure in her domain, brought a wealth of experience, ranging from strategic philanthropy and fund development to mentorship in geriatric care and transformative work in community engagement.

The uniqueness of their collaboration lies in the collective wisdom distilled into this book. It offers not just individual narratives, but a tapestry of experiences woven together, highlighting the power of collective insight and the impact of diverse leadership styles. Their stories, rich in expertise and inspiration, provide a compelling exploration of what it means to lead with purpose, passion, and a relentless drive to make a difference.

This book stands as a testament to the power of collaboration, and the extraordinary potential that emerges when dynamic women leaders unite their voices for a common cause.

Listen to the podcast!